I0003402

UNIX
From Soup To Nuts

Robert B. Fay

Copyright © 2010 Robert B. Fay

All rights reserved.

ISBN-10: 1456507281
ISBN-13: 978-1456507282

DEDICATION

To my wife, Alayna, and my kids, Dakota and Kiana.
May life continue to bring you success and happiness.

CONTENTS

ACKNOWLEDGMENTS

Robert would like to thank L.D. Barthlome for talking him into applying for his first position as a UNIX System Administrator. Additionally, Robert would like to thank Rick Parker, Lynn Harris, and Gordon Howell for the opportunity to make the switch from RPG programmer to UNIX System Administrator and Database Administrator. The ability to make that switch in career path opened new doors of opportunity. Robert would like to offer special thanks to his friend and study partner Susan Mock for her many hours of proof reading and editing.

1 UNIX BASICS

This book is intended for users of UNIX and Linux operating systems. However, throughout the body of this text, the discussions refer to the UNIX operating system unless a feature is being discussed that is unique to a distribution of the Linux operating system. My intent is to introduce basic and vital concepts that must be grasped by both users and Systems Administrators of UNIX operating systems alike. I have included topics found in beginner UNIX training courses up through intermediate-level System Administration courses.

This book is not intended to be a System Administration manual. Rather, it is intended to be a road map to introduce UNIX users to utilities, commands, protocols, and programs found on UNIX operating systems. It is written in a fashion to provide concepts that build on each other. Each chapter or main subject area will include a table of common command or utility options along with some syntax examples and sample output. Additionally, at the end of each chapter are a few opportunities for you to exercise what you have just learned. The solutions to the chapter exercises are provided in the back of this book. I do not recommend that you skip around too much the first time through reading this book. After your initial read, I hope you will find this book useful as a handy, easy-to-use reference.

Conventions Used in This Book

The following is a list of conventions provided to help you understand the verbiage used in the examples in this book as well as other mainstream UNIX documentation sources. I have used industry standard methods and conventions to assist you to seamlessly read this book and try lessons learned on a UNIX machine without having to translate anything. I believe you will find that the lessons contained in this book are directly portable to mainstream UNIX and Linux operating systems.

- . – Dot. The dot is not to be confused with the period. The dot is used to identify an invisible file. If a filename begins with a dot, then the file will not show up when files are listed unless you specify to show you invisible files. The dot is also used to identify locations in a directory. One dot means the current directory. Two dots mean the directory directly above where you are in the directory tree.
- file - Is a reference to a file. This is where a file goes in the syntax of a command.
- filename - Means to insert the name of your file here.
- file.out - This is the output file from whatever syntax it is preceded by.
- infile - This is the input file for a command.
- " " - Double quotes. Whatever is in between the double quotes is a literal.
- # - Pound sign. This is known in the UNIX world as a hash mark. Everything to the right of this is a comment and not code. The hash mark is also commonly used as the command prompt for the root user, but this is not a system requirement. The examples in this book begin with a # symbol to indicate that I am running these commands at the command prompt. You do not need to type the # symbol when you are trying these examples out on your UNIX system. If you do, you will get an error.
- ! - Exclamation mark or exclamation point. This is known in the UNIX world as a bang symbol. The bang symbol is used in place of the word "not" as in not equal to in a comparison statement.
- Environment Variables - Are in all capital letters.
- / - Slash. All slashes are forward slashes / in a directory tree. (The opposite of Microsoft Windows operating systems.)
- Blank Lines - Blank lines and other white space in a file are ignored.

- [] – Square braces. The first time a new UNIX command is introduced in this book, it will be surrounded by square braces so you can pick them out more easily in a sentence.
- () – Parentheses. Comments and examples are enclosed in parentheses.
- Tables – When I talk about tables, I am talking about a chart like a spreadsheet that contains related information in formatted columns with headers.

File Extensions

A *file extension* is the letters that follow the last dot in a file name. Strictly speaking, UNIX does not care how a file is named. But certain applications may depend on a file extension-naming convention. Since there are so many types of file extensions, I have only included some of the more common types you are likely to see on a UNIX operating system.

If you are using a Linux operating system, you may notice that file names are displayed with different color letters depending on what type of file they are. Some examples are as follows: An executable file will be green, a directory will be dark blue, and a tar file will be red. This behavior is controlled with the variable called LS_COLORS. I have purposely omitted graphics files from the list because you cannot manually edit them from the command line. One change that I always make to a Linux environment when I login is to change the LS_COLORS entry for directories to 00 (di=00). This will change the colors of the letters from dark blue on a black background to white letters on a black background. I think this is much easier to read and it demonstrates your ability to manipulate the environment based on file types.

Common File Extensions	
Extension	**Description**
.bak	Backup File
.c	c source code file
.c++	c++ source code file
.cf	Configuration file

3

.cnf	Configuration file
.conf	Configuration file
.dat	Data file
.db	Database file
.dbf	Database file
.err	Error log file
.gif	Graphics Interchange Format file
.gz	Gzipped file
.htm	Hypertext markup language file
.html	Hypertext markup language file
.idx	Index file
.jar	Java archive file
.ksh	Korn shell script file
.lic	License file
.lock	System lock file
.log	Log file
.out	Output file from a script
.pl	Perl script file
.sh	Shell script file
.tar	Tape archive file
.txt	Text file

.war	Java web archive file
.Z	Compressed file
.zip	Zipped file

Common Directory Names

Certain directory names are used in more than one location in UNIX. You may also see them used within applications that run on UNIX platforms. This standardization allows us to intuitively know where to look for and where to put certain types of files. The following list includes the names and descriptions of common directories.

Common Directory Names	
Name	**Description**
bin	This is a directory that holds executable files, utilities, and ready-to-run programs that the system needs to boot. Think of this as a physical storage bin.
dev	This directory holds files that support devices.
etc	This is a directory that holds configuration files. Do not mess around in here until you know what you are doing. At the very least, make a copy of any configuration file before you edit it. At some point in the future, you will be glad you adopted the practice of making copies before changing something.
home	This is a directory full of sub-directories. There should be a sub-directory for every user that has an account on the system. The user's home directory is where the user will be placed when they log on to the system. The home directory is where users should store all of their personal files.

lib	This is a library directory. Think of it as a physical library but for programs. You remember libraries, the place we used to go for information before the Internet.
lost+found	This is where files are recovered to by fsck (the file system check utility) after file system corruption is detected. This directory is normally empty.
proc	This directory has a collection of files that each holds different types of system information. For example, the cpuinfo file contains information about systems processors.
sbin	This directory is very similar to the bin directory. It holds executables and utilities. The difference is that sbin holds things that only the root or administrative users should have access to. For this reason, sbin is not put in a user's $PATH variable by default.
temp	This is a temporary directory. Do not put things in here that you need to keep. Things in this directory may disappear after the system is rebooted.
tmp	This is a temporary directory. Do not put things in here that you need to keep. Things in this directory may disappear after the system is rebooted.
usr	This is a directory that holds system binaries and applications. Most people pronounce the directors like "user," but there is not user information stored here. The name usr is actually an acronym that stands for UNIX Shared Resources.
var	This is the variable area of the operating environment. I am not sure if that is what the creators of UNIX had in mind when they called it var, but it seems to fit, so that is what I tell myself. What I mean by variable is that things in var are always changing. This area holds mail queues, print queues, logs… You get the idea. Don't let var get

	full by a log or mailbox going unchecked. If it fills up, your operating system will not be able to write logs and you will soon notice a performance problem or perhaps experience an unexpected reboot. Normally this is not a problem, but it happens. A good system administrator will have monitoring scripts running to send alerts when things start to fill up and perhaps automatically prune logs.
/	The forward slash by itself is the symbol for the root directory. The root directory is that base of the entire UNIX operating system. All parts of the UNIX operating system use this point as the beginning of their absolute path. The easy way to remember this is to think of the UNIX operating system as a tree. The / "root" directory is the root for the tree.

Standards

Although UNIX is considered to be an open system, there are still certain standards that are followed by vendors and developers. Adhering to these standards helps to insure the portability of applications and utilities between different UNIX platforms and distributions. Beginning in the late 1980s, an open operating system standardization effort now known as POSIX provided a common baseline for all operating systems; IEEE based POSIX around the common structure of the major competing variants of the UNIX system, publishing the first POSIX standard in 1988. At around the same time, a separate but very similar standard known as the Single UNIX Specification was produced by the Open Group. The following groups have been formed to develop standards for UNIX.

UNIX Standards Organizations	
Group Name	**Description**
GNU	GNU Not UNIX (Free Linux)

ISO	International Standards Organization
OSF	Open Software Foundation
POSIX	Portable Operating System Interface
SVID	System V Interface Description
XOPEN	A consortium of international computer vendors that was founded in 1984 to resolve standards issues. X/Open merged with the Open Software Foundation in 1996 to become The Open Group.
The Open Group	A vendor-neutral and technology-neutral consortium formed to develop open source standards.

Introduction to UNIX

The name *UNIX* refers to a computer operating system that was originally developed in the late 1960s to early 1970s by a group at AT&T's Bell Labs. The motivation that was the driving factor behind the creating of the UNIX operating system was the requirement for a multi-user, multi-tasking operating system for programmers.

The job of an operating system is to control system hardware like the processor, memory, and disk drives to perform useful tasks. When you want the computer to do something for you, like start a program, copy a file, or display the contents of a directory, it is the operating system that must perform those tasks for you.

The philosophy behind the design of UNIX was to provide simple yet powerful utilities that could be pieced together in a manner to perform a wide variety of tasks. The following example demonstrates how three UNIX commands are used together to generate a detailed listing, narrow the output with a filter to view only the desired files, and arrange them in alphabetical order by name. (ls –al | grep txt | sort –k 9)

I don't want to get ahead of myself too much by explaining commands or code syntax yet, but suffice it to say that the previous example uses three UNIX commands, three command options, two redirection pipes, and a search argument. Sound complicated? Well, it will all make sense soon. The important things to remember are that UNIX is full of commands that are easy to use, the commands have options that can change their behavior, and the commands can be used together to increase the efficiency of the task you are performing.

The names most commonly credited to the development of the first UNIX operating system are Dennis Ritchie, Douglas McIlroy, and Ken Thompson. The name UNIX has since been trademarked as UNIX in all capital letters. The current owner of the trademark is The Open Group, which is a consortium that sets the standards to be used in the development of UNIX operating systems. The name UNIX is not an acronym; rather, it follows the naming convention used for the old Big Iron computers that dictates names will consist of all capital letters.

The Open Group has decided that systems must be compliant and certified to adhere to their Single UNIX Specification, which they have developed in order to be called UNIX. All other systems, which are close but are not certified, must be called UNIX-like systems. You may be familiar with or at least have heard of some of the more popular UNIX-like operating systems. Linux is one of these systems that have gained a tremendous amount of popularity recently due to its user friendliness and its ability to run on the Intel platform.

Modern implementations of UNIX and UNIX-like systems have separated into various groups or classes. These different versions of UNIX have been developed by commercial vendors, universities, and other not-for-profit organizations. Those in the UNIX community commonly refer to the different types of UNIX as flavors. Various flavors of UNIX have been deployed extensively on hardware ranging from enterprise class servers to notebook computers.

The bigger players (vendors) sometimes also develop their own flavor of UNIX so that it can only be used on their hardware or chip design. Some of the more popular and robust chipsets UNIX runs on include IBM's RISC (Reduced Instruction Set Computer) and SUN's SPARC (Scalable Processor

Architecture). While the many flavors of Linux are gaining favor because of their ability to run on the less-expensive Intel chipset, companies are discovering that they can build a clustered Linux environment for a much smaller investment in hardware than they used to spend on the large enterprise class servers of yesteryear. The following list includes some of the vendors that have developed their own flavor of UNIX or UNIX-like operating system.

Vendors of UNIX or UNIX-Like Platforms		
Common Name	**Vendor Name**	**Flavor of UNIX**
BSD	Berkley Software Development	FreeBSD
BSD	Berkley Software Development	NetBSD
BSD	Berkley Software Development	OpenBSD
HP	Hewlett Packard	HP-UX
IBM	International Business Machines	AIX
Mac	Macintosh	Mac OS X
Novell	Novell	SuSE Linux
SCO	The SCO Group	UNIXWare
SUN	Stanford University Network	Solaris
SUN	Stanford University Network	Solaris x86
SUN	Stanford University Network	SunOS
Redhat	Redhat	Linux

UNIX was designed to be portable, multi-tasking, and multi-user in a time-sharing configuration. UNIX systems are characterized by various concepts: the use of plain text for storing data; a hierarchical file system; treating devices and certain types of inter-process communication (IPC) as files; and the use of a large number of small programs that can be strung together through a command line interpreter using pipes, as opposed to using a single monolithic program that includes all of the same functionality. These concepts are known as the UNIX philosophy.

A few things that are not part of the UNIX philosophy would be an intuitive interface, requirement for graphics or graphics hardware, and mouse functionality. These things are all available for UNIX platforms, but the UNIX operating system itself does not need them nor does an experienced UNIX user. In the UNIX world, these items are considered to be luxuries or frills. Personally, I would rather not mess with them. I do not need them to do my job, and they use system resources that I would rather have devoted to something else. The exception, of course, is if you are using your UNIX platform as a gaming server. If that is the case, then load that sucker up with memory and the best graphics hardware you can get a driver for and go to town.

Of course, you can always write your own driver files, but that subject is beyond the scope of this book. Perhaps in volume two of this book we will be able to discus subjects like writing custom drivers to accommodate hardware that the kernel does not know about. After all, that is essentially what a driver does. It describes to the kernel what a particular hardware device is so it knows what to do with it and how to communicate with it.

Where UNIX Got Its Name

"Where does the name UNIX come from?" you may ask. Well, in the 1960s, AT&T, General Electric (GE), and the Massachusetts Institute of Technology (MIT) worked on a collaborative effort to develop an operating system called the Multiplexed Information and Computing Service (Multics), which ran on GE's mainframe computer. The Multics project never realized much commercial success primarily because of its poor performance, but its development generated new capabilities for interactive systems, like enhanced security features.

After the Multics project was over, AT&T committed its development resources to a new project. The project was called the Uniplexed Information and Computing System (Unics). A developer by the name of Brian Kernighan has been credited for the name Unics, but I think we can definitely agree that it is a play on the name of the Multics project. The spelling was later changed to UNIX.

The Rosetta Stone

The Rosetta stone has Egyptian and Greek writing on it. The writings were made using Hieroglyphic, Demotic, and Greek script. It was written in three scripts because when it was written, there were three scripts being used in Egypt. The Hieroglyphic script was used for important documents like those with religious significance. The Demotic script was the common script of Egypt. Greek was the language of the rulers of Egypt at that time. The Rosetta stone was written in all three scripts so that the priests, government officials, and rulers of Egypt could all read it. It could also be used as a translation tool because it contains the same writings in different languages and scripts. Therefore, if you can read at least one of the scripts, you can make at least an educated guess as to what the characters in the other scripts represent.

Okay, so you are probably saying to yourself, this is all very interesting, but what does it have to do with UNIX? Well, since there are so many flavors of UNIX out there, it has become necessary to develop translation documents to assist with the ability to perform common tasks on different flavors of UNIX. It is quite common to find data centers with servers made by different vendors supporting different flavors of UNIX in the same environment. These translation documents may be found in many forms, but they are collectively referred to as *Rosetta stones*.

A quick search on the Internet with your search engine of choice should respond with several choices of Rosetta stone documents, or at least enough information to assist you in creating your own. Try searching for "UNIX Rosetta stone" and see what you get. I just tried it and got 97,000 hits. The number-one hit was a Java script in which you could choose from a list of 17 flavors of UNIX to compare.

If you have experience with another operating system like DOS or PIC, you may find it useful to find or create a Rosetta stone document to translate those commands to UNIX. This will be useful until you start thinking in the new OS you are learning. I know for a while I knew how to do things easily off the top of my head with AIX commands. I would then have to go translate them into Solaris commands to get something accomplished on a SUN or Fujitsu server. Many commands are universal between flavors of UNIX, but sometimes they have different options available.

UNIX Versus Popular Operating Systems with Graphical Windows

Since most of us who are endeavoring to enhance our knowledge of computers and operating systems are already reasonably comfortable with our ability to use a personal computer running a Microsoft Windows operating system, it seems sensible to include a brief comparison between UNIX and Microsoft Windows. This is not intended to be a Windows bashing session. Nor is it intended to be a lecture about how UNIX is better than Windows. I just thought now would be a good time to bring your attention to some features that are generally recognized to be true about the two types of operating systems as far as strengths and weaknesses go. However, I wish to be clear that I am only presenting these items as matters of my own opinion. You, of course, are welcome to form your own opinion if you have not done so already.

The UNIX operating system is a multi-user and multi-tasking environment. What I mean by that is that any number of people can be logged into a UNIX machine doing independent tasks while sharing the system resources. UNIX has many layers of built-in security features. These features not only restrict people from logging in to a UNIX machine, they also govern what a person can do while logged in. UNIX is what is known as an open system. The term open system refers to the ability to make changes to the operating system that will change its behavior as well as the user's environment. UNIX is able to run on multiple hardware platforms, it is reliable and robust, and it provides an excellent back end for heavy transaction applications like databases, data warehouses, web hosting, and analytical and scientific applications.

The Microsoft Windows operating system is a single-user environment. It has what most people would call a user-friendly interface. It is relatively easy to learn how to use. It is the market leading operating system for personal computers. It is easy to get compatible software for and is easy to install. All that being said, don't expect to go to Berkley or Stanford and impress people because you can change your wallpaper on your Windows desktop.

Parts and Pieces

The UNIX operating system is comprised of essentially three main parts: The Kernel, the standard utility programs, and the system configuration files. There are other goodies that come with it and there is plenty that can be added to it, to be sure, but the three aforementioned parts are what make up the original portable operating system.

The Kernel

The *Kernel* is the core of the UNIX operating system. Basically, the Kernel is a large program (sometimes referred to as the master control program) that is loaded into memory when the machine is turned on. The Kernel controls the allocation of hardware resources from boot time until shutdown. The Kernel knows what hardware resources are available, and it has the necessary programs, a.k.a. drivers, to talk to all the devices connected to it. One of the most important high-level tasks the Kernel performs is the scheduling of devices access. This is necessary to prevent two programs from trying to gain control of a device simultaneously. The Kernel has special rights granted to it to use system resources that users do not have access to. This is known as overhead and defines the division between user space and system space.

Originally the Kernel was located in /usr/sys and contained several sub-components located in various sub-directories. The configuration files were located in /usr/sys/conf, and the device drivers were located in /usr/sys/dev, and so on. You get the idea. The structure of UNIX has changed substantially since the original version. Having been through a complete re-write to the C programming language and versions developed by different vendors over the years, chances are the above layout of the Kernel probably does not apply to the version you are using. Incidentally, as you read the name /usr to yourself, you are probably pronouncing it like "user," which is generally accepted as the correct pronunciation. But be aware that this directory does not contain your user information. I have made it a point to present this information twice in this book in different ways because it is very important. System users should not be messing around in the /usr section of the operating system. Doing so without due cause may be detrimental to your operating system. The /usr directory is actually an acronym for UNIX shared resources. This is where most of your commands live.

Utility Programs

The *utility programs* are really the core of the UNIX command set. These programs include simple utilities, like email and word processing, as well as complex utilities, like the shell that allows you to issue commands to the operating system. There are not clearly defined sub-categories of UNIX utilities, because UNIX was designed for programmers in mind and as such is not as intuitive as operating systems that were designed with the general public in mind.

Some utility programs are definitely used for system or administrative functions, like mkfs to make new filesystems or fsck to check the status and integrity of filesystems. You will know if a utility is for system use rather than for the general population of users if you try to run one while logged in as a user other than the root user; the operating system will respond with a message like "mkfs: Operation not allowed" or something equally as rude. The system messages are not very friendly, but they get their point across. They can be very useful once you learn how to read them. Sometimes they point you right to the problem. The previous one, for example, tells me that I am not allowed to use the mkfs command. In other words, the user I am logged in as has inadequate permissions to access or execute the mkfs file or command. Remember to UNIX, everything is a file.

System Configuration Files

The *system configuration files* are a set of files that provide instructions to the kernel and utility programs. The kernel and the utility programs read the configuration files at startup to decide how to behave during execution time. The UNIX kernel and utilities are flexible programs, and certain aspects of their behavior can be controlled. The configuration files are the medium you can use to exercise this control. Since the kernel and utility programs read the configuration files at startup, it usually takes a reboot of the system or a restart of a service or utility program process before the changes to the configuration files are noticed and the changes are implemented. It should be noted that start up means different things for the kernel than it does for a utility program.

To the kernel, startup means to reboot the operating system. While it is possible to make the kernel refresh itself by rereading the configuration files, it is much easier to reboot the entire operating system. However, make sure you understand what the changes to the kernel will affect before you implement them. I recommend making any system changes on a test system first. As a matter of fact, when you are testing a new kernel parameter, you should not only verify that the system reboots successfully, you should also verify that all of the normal application functions still work for a while. Sometimes it can take a bit for problems to show up after a configuration change.

To utility programs, startup or restarting is much simpler than when dealing with the system Kernel. The operating system will chug along just fine whether or not most utility programs are running. Therefore, you can shut down a utility program or the service it provides independent of the operating system. In other words, leave the operating system running and just kill the utility program. Then use the normal startup process to reinitialize and start the utility program. If it starts up, monitor it for a while to verify the old functionality you wanted to keep is still there, as well as to verify that the changes you made have accomplished the desired results.

One example of a system configuration file is the *filesystem table*. The filesystem table is named differently depending on what version of the UNIX or Linux operating system you are running. Some of the systems I have used call the filesystem table names like [vfstab], [fstab], or [filesystems]. The filesystem table is a configuration file that tells the Kernel where to mount all of the filesystems on the disk drives as well as when to mount them. Another example is the system log configuration file [syslog.conf], which tells the Kernel how to record the various kinds of events and errors it may encounter. The filesystem table and the syslog.conf file can be found in the /etc directory.

Protocols

A *protocol* is a set of rules that the operating system must use to communicate with other computers. By adhering to the protocol standards, computers understand the format of the communication for a given task. For example, Hypertext Transfer Protocol (HTTP) outlines the rules for a computer's web browser to interpret files it is accessing on a server so that it can accurately display a web page on your monitor when the server responds to your request for a page.

The following table lists some common protocols you may have already become familiar with or will surely encounter in your dealings on a UNIX computer. A more complete list of protocols can be viewed in the [protocols] file located at /etc/inet/protocols. A list of services supported by these protocols can be viewed in the [services] file located at /etc/inet/services.

Protocols	
Acronym	**Description**
FC	Fibre Channel
FTP	File Transfer Protocol
HTTP	Hypertext Transfer Protocol
ICMP	Internet Control Message Protocol
IP	Internet Protocol
LDAP	Lightweight Directory Access Protocol
NTP	Network Time Protocol

POP	Post Office Protocol
TCP	Transmission Control Protocol
UDP	User Datagram Protocol

You may or may not have noticed the difference with the Fibre Channel protocol at the beginning of the previous table. While it is a valid protocol that I use regularly, you probably will not deal with this unless you are managing a storage area network (SAN). The reason I added FC to the list of protocols was to make you aware that not all protocol acronyms end with "P". Most of them do, but it is not an industry requirement. Additionally, for those of you that have not dealt with a SAN or fibre optics, the correct spelling for fibre channel is "fibre" and not "fiber". The spell checker does not like fibre, but that is the way it is. If you want fiber, go have a bran muffin.

Services

A *service* is a tool or function of the operating system that makes something available to you. Most services in a UNIX environment are related to networking or system security. For example, the Domain Name Service (DNS) translates human recognizable names to IP addresses and vice versa. This is a useful service for networking between two or more computers because the operating system uses IP addresses to identify computers, but it is much easier for people to remember names like Web_Server or Jupiter than an IP address like 192.168.10.1. The following table identifies services that are available on UNIX systems.

UNIX Services	
Acronym / Name	**Description**
mail	Email service
news	Print news items
dns	Domain name service

nfs	Network file service
nis	Network information name service
whois	Internet user name directory service

The Shell

The *shell* is a command programming language that provides an interface for users to communicate with and make requests from the UNIX operating system. Before window systems were developed, the shell was the only interface available to UNIX users. The /etc/shells file will list all of the shells available for your system. If this is not the exact location on your system, the file should still be called shells or some variation of the word "shell". The following illustration demonstrates the shell's role as a barrier of protection from the users. Like a physical shell or wall if you will, the UNIX shell protects what is inside from being damaged or affected by what is going on outside. The shell is a good thing. The shell is there for a reason.

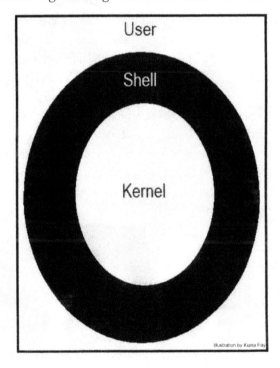

The following table lists common shells found on UNIX systems:

Common UNIX Shells		
Description	Absolute Path	Shell
Bash shell	/usr/bin/bash	bash
Bourne shell	/usr/bin/sh	sh
C shell	/usr/bin/csh	csh
Korn shell	/usr/bin/ksh	ksh
Tcsh shell	/usr/bin/tcsh	tcsh
Zsh shell	/usr/bin/zsh	zsh

There is usually more than one way to perform a task in UNIX. You will develop preferences for certain methods that may be different than your co-workers. That is fine as long as you remember neither way is necessarily the only or best method for the job. To demonstrate this concept, I have listed three different methods of displaying what shell I am using. All three of the methods accomplish the task of telling me what shell I am running. All three methods are about the same amount of keystrokes. So in this case it is all a matter of my personal preference as to which command syntax to use. In other situations, different methods may use drastically different amounts of keystrokes. Given that situation, I will almost always opt for the fewer keystrokes method, as I have never been very fast at the keyboard. However, I comfort myself by noticing that folks who type really fast are wasting many of their keystrokes by constantly hitting the backspace key to correct what they mistyped.

#echo $SHELL

#env | grep SHELL

#set | grep SHELL

The preceding commands will give you slightly different output, but they will all include the value of your current shell environment variable. To change your active shell, you need to change the value of your shell environment variable and then export the variable. The [export] part tells the system to re-read the specified environment variable and implement it. To change your shell to bash from some other shell, you should execute the following command syntax:

#export SHELL=/usr/bin/bash

The change in shells will not be immediately apparent until you try to use one of the shell's exclusive features. Try one of the previous commands to see that your shell has changed.

The operating system will allow you to run multiple nested shells. However, when you set up shell variables, they will not be available in a nested shell. To return to the previous shell, just type "exit" and hit the return key once. Warning: Keep track of how many shells or sub-shells you are running or you can log out of the operating system when trying to exit from one shell to the next.

Standard Input and Output

Standard input and output, or I/O as it is called, refers to the user interface. Standard input comes from the keyboard and or mouse if you are using a graphical interface, and standard output goes to the screen. Other types of input and output can come from or go to commands, files, and other devices.

The output from one command can be used as the input to another command. The following command syntax example shows how the output of one command becomes the input to the next command. The " | " character is called a *pipe*. Just like a pipe in the plumbing of your house it, transports something from one place to another. Only in this case we are using our pipe to transport data instead of water.

Data flows through pipes from left to right. So the output from the command to the left of the pipe becomes the input for the command to the right of the pipe. Go ahead and try the following command. It is harmless. Without getting too far ahead of ourselves, I'll tell you that this command will display active process information one page at a time. Use the enter key to advance through the pages. If you are using a system that does not have the pg command, substitute the "more" command in its place.

```
#ps –ef | pg
#ps –ef | more
```

Getting Started

Connecting To and Accessing UNIX

There are a couple of ways you can access a UNIX system. The main mode of access to a UNIX machine is through a terminal. A *terminal* includes a keyboard and a video monitor. For each terminal connected to the UNIX system, the Kernel runs a process called a *tty* that accepts input from the terminal and sends output to the terminal. The tty processes are utility programs, and they must be told the capabilities of the terminal in order to correctly read from, and write to, the terminal. If the tty process receives incorrect information about the terminal type, unexpected results can occur. To display the current terminal type, enter the following syntax at the command prompt:

```
#echo $TERM
```

To change your current terminal type to vt100, enter the following syntax at the command prompt:

```
#export TERM=vt100
```

I have found that vt100 or vt220 is the correct emulation for terminal emulation programs running on personal computers. If you are using just a dumb terminal, than you should be able to tell the operating system exactly what kind of display you are using. It should say on the front of the monitor what type of display it is. If not, the old "wyse60" seems to work on many old dumb terminals. The wyse60 emulation mimics the appearance of a Wyse model 60 terminal, which is popular because of its high-resolution character cell that displays nice crisp characters. You will appreciate the high-resolution characters when you are pulling an all-nighter because someone promised you would deliver something on an unreasonable schedule, and you get left holding the bag.

The System Console

The *console* is a special type of terminal that is recognized when the system is started. Some UNIX system operations must be performed at the console. Typically, the console is only accessible by the system administrator. Facilities that have large numbers of rack-mounted servers often do not have room for a physical console to be attached to each server individually. For this reason, some vendors have incorporated into their hardware design a port that can be accessed either by way of a management network connection or a temporary laptop connection. I say temporary because the console does not need to be connected for UNIX to perform its functions. It is just required in the event that maintenance or some type of failure prohibits remote connection.

SUN Microsystems has developed what is known as a LOM (Lights Out Management) port on their systems. The LOM port will remain functional even if the operating system is down as long as power is connected to the server. The LOM connection will allow the system administrator to perform maintenance when the system is not fully functional or when network connectivity is not available. Other versions of the LOM interface are the ALOM or Advanced LOM and the ILOM or Integrated LOM. Other hardware vendors have developed similar technology for communicating with a server without an active operating system, but SUN is one of the big players in the UNIX arena.

For facilities that have large numbers of rack-mounted servers that do not have room for a physical console to be attached to each server individually and do not have a Lights Out Management network configured, another solution is the "crash cart". Similar to a hospital crash cart that is highly mobile and contains devices typically needed for a patient in cardiac arrest or some other medical emergency, a data center crash cart has the things a server needs to save it quickly. A data center crash cart typically has a display, keyboard, mouse, box of cables, and set of tools on it. The idea is that if a server goes down unexpectedly, the crash cart can be used to quickly gain console access to the server to determine why the server went down and resolve the problem. A crash cart can also be used to configure new servers that do not have an operating system installed or network connectivity configured yet.

Dumb Terminals

Some terminals are referred to as "dumb" terminals because they only have the ability to send characters as input to the UNIX system and receive characters as output from the UNIX system. They cannot execute programs or perform any computing on their own. Personal computers are often used to emulate dumb terminals, so that they can be connected to a UNIX system. Dumb terminals can be connected directly to a UNIX machine or may be connected remotely, through a modem or a terminal server.

Since everybody has some sort of computer workstation on their desk these days, the most popular way to connect to remote UNIX systems is with emulation programs. There are plenty to choose from. Many are free and some are not. I use the same free program at work and at home. It is called "putty," and I recommend it highly. The price is right, you can customize and save your session parameters, and it has different connection methods available, including ssh, which is required by most security-conscious organizations. To obtain a copy of putty, just search for it with your favorite Internet search engine. It is small and portable. I carry around a copy of putty on a flash drive so I have access to the environment I am used to working in with little to no setup before I get started. I also keep a copy on a CD in the disaster recovery bins at work. This is a good idea, because you never know if you will be able to download stuff from the Internet following a disaster.

Smart Terminals

Smart terminals, like the X terminal, can interact with the UNIX system at a higher level. Smart terminals have enough on-board memory and processing power to support graphical interfaces. The interaction between a smart terminal and a UNIX system can go beyond simple characters to include icons, windows, menus, and mouse actions. With the right software loaded, a personal computer can emulate a smart terminal as well. Some vendors manufacture thin clients, which give the appearance of a smart terminal.

A *thin client* is a small-footprint, low-power consumption device that you connect your monitor, keyboard, mouse and network cable to as if it were the UNIX machine itself. The difference is a thin client sits on your desktop and only takes a few square inches of space, depending on the make and model you get. Thin clients are a good choice for cost-sensitive environments with many connections to a UNIX environment, like a call center. The thin client communicates with a master server that provides the UNIX functionality to all of the thin clients on the network. Each thin client then uses its borrowed UNIX functionality to perform tasks and make connections to other UNIX servers on the network. To each user of a thin client, the environment is presented as if they have their own UNIX computer on their desktop but for a fraction of the price and at a greatly reduced power consumption or cooling impact. Thin client devices generate virtually no heat signature.

Aliases

The [alias] mechanism is available to create a user-defined identifier to a command or list of commands that will be executed when the identifier is used at the command line. Simply stated, the *alias command* allows a user to remember a single word or command that is used to execute a more complicated or more difficult to remember command syntax. A common alias I have seen used on many UNIX operating systems is for the df command. The df command is almost always executed with a common option like –k or –h, depending on the user's personal preference. So, when a user creates an alias of df for the command syntax df –h, the user will just need to type df at the command line and the system will run df –h. Obviously this example is not a difficult to remember command syntax, rather the alias is used to save three key strokes whenever the frequently used df –h command is executed. As simple as the previous example is, I believe a UNIX user will understand how powerful the alias command can be to save time, key strokes, and the need to memorize complicated commands.

The alias command can be used to display the aliases that are active in the current shell and how the aliases are defined. To view the defined aliases, simply execute the alias command by itself without any arguments. If an alias is defined incorrectly, or if you simply want to remove an alias, use the [unalias] command. The argument you must provide the unalias command is the name of the alias you would like to remove. An alias that is defined in a session will only be available for that particular login session unless the user defines the alias within their .profile file in their home directory.

Anything defined within a user's .profile will be defined every time the user logs into the system. Additionally, if all users need to have the same alias defined, the system administrator may define the alias for all users. This task can be performed in different ways depending on the system administrator's preference and the flavor of UNIX being used. A common way to perform this task would be to insert the alias definition into the /etc/profile file. This file is read by the operating system every time someone logs into the system. The following two examples demonstrate how to properly define an alias for a single command as well as how to define an alias for a command string.

#alias newcommand=oldcommand

#alias newcommand='old command string'

Rules for Entering UNIX Commands

Wildcards

The following special characters are called *wildcards*. They can be used to list or search for multiple files at the same time, which can save you a ton of typing and time. If you learn to use your wildcards effectively, you will be a much happier and more efficient UNIX user.

Wildcard Symbols	
Wildcard	**Description**
?	Matches any single character.
*	Matches any single character or multiple characters.
[]	Matches one of the characters included inside the [ ] symbols.

The following are some examples for using the above wildcards:

#ls stuff?

26

The above command will list any file in the current directory that begins with the word "stuff" followed by one more character. So if the following files were in the current directory, they would show up in the results (stuff1, stuffs, stuffy). Some files that would not show up in the results are (stuff11, stuffed, stufff). These file names do not qualify for the list because they start with the word stuff and then have more than one character. If the command syntax had called for two question marks like (stuff??) then the three files that did not qualify would have qualified for the list but the original three files that qualified would not have. The three original files that qualified would no longer qualify because (stuff??) calls for any two more characters and not one or two.

#ls stuff*

The above command will list any file in the current directory that begins with the word "stuff." So all of the file names in the following list qualify (stuff, stuff1, stuffs, stuffy, stuff11, stuffed, stufff). The asterisk character accepts any additional characters or none at all.

#ls stuff[1,2,y,z]

The above command will list any file in the current directory that begins with the word "stuff" followed by one more character that is included in the square braces. So if the following files were in the current directory, they would show up in the results (stuff1, stuff2, stuffy, stuffz). Some files that would not show up in the results are (stuff11, stuff3, stuffy1). These file names do not qualify for the list because they start with the word "stuff" and then have more than one character or a character that is not included in the square braces.

Command Options, Arguments, and Required Spaces

Options are supported variations of a command. Options are specified by entering a space after a command followed by a dash "-" (most of the time) and the desired option character. I say most of the time, because most commands require the dash, but not all of them do. However, the commands that do not require the dash will allow it without complaining, so the safe bet is to always include the dash.

An option character for one command may be used for a different purpose with a different command. Another popular term you may hear among UNIX users is the word "flag." A command flag and a command option are the same thing. Either term is acceptable and is regularly used interchangeably. If somebody does not know what you are talking about when you say the word "flag" when referring to a UNIX command option, please have them escorted out of the data center before they break something. They do not belong near a system console.

Example: In the command string (su –c oracle), the c means run the following command as the oracle user. In the command string (tar –cvf file file.tar), the c means to create a tar file.

An *argument* is the subject or target of the command. It is entered last on the command line following the command and any options. Spaces must be included between commands, options, and arguments in order for the operating system to interpret them correctly.

Exception: Spaces are not required between options if multiple options are specified and only the first option needs to be preceded by a dash character (-).

Man (Manual) Pages

The [man] command can display a "man page" for every command on the system, including itself. The man pages are documentation you have access to at the UNIX command line. UNIX was the first operating system to include all of its documentation online in machine and human readable format. So use it. That is what it is there for. You will be glad it is there and that you know how to use it some day when you are trying to figure something out and that person that sits in the cube across the hall who you always ask questions is not available. The documentation included:

man — Manual pages for each command, library component, system call, header file, etc.

doc — Longer documents detailing major subsystems, such as the C language and troff.

The man pages are the most convenient and complete source for getting help on a UNIX operating system. To use the man pages, enter the command "man" on the command line followed by a space and an argument. In this case, the argument would be the UNIX command, protocol, or service you want help with. The man page will respond by listing several pages of output that consists of the following sections:

man Page Information by Section	
Command	**The Command You Looked Up**
Name	The command followed by a description of what it is used for.
Synopsis	An example of the syntax the command is used in.
Description	A more verbose description of what the command is used for and how to use it.
Options	A definition of each option supported for the command.
Operands	Types of arguments that may be specified with the command like a file or a pattern.
Usage	Examples of how to use the command.
Environment Variables	A list of environment variables that can affect the execution of the command.
Exit Status	Possible exit status codes.
Attributes	Characteristics of the command.
Files	Files that are related to the current command being looked up.
Notes	Notes of useful information from the author of the command.

Bugs	Known issues or "bugs" at the time the current version of the operating system was published.

Man pages are a very valuable resource that can continue to help you as you learn the UNIX operating system. However, man page entries usually contain way more information than you need. Don't be afraid to browse man pages to find what you need and then move on.

A great way to find what you are looking for is the vi search function. Once you have opened the man page, type a single forward slash character without hitting the return key. The system is now waiting for you to enter a search word. Type something you want to search for and hit the return key. The system will jump to the first occurrence of the search word in the man page. If you want to jump to the next occurrence, just hit the "n" key and you will be off to the next occurrence. To back up one screen if you get overzealous with your n's, just hit the "b" key. To learn more about how to use the man page, use man to look up man. Also, learn to use the vi navigation functions. Reading man pages in their entirety can be very time-consuming and boring.

Command Not Found Errors

The *command not found error* is very common. It usually means that you either spelled the desired command incorrectly or it is not in your $PATH. If you do not normally need the command in your path, you can execute it by entering the absolute path of the command. If you are sitting in the directory where the executable file resides, you can execute it by preceding it with a dot and a forward slash "./file". The preceding trick only works to help you execute a command that your $PATH cannot find but you have the proper permissions to execute the file. Executing the command from the local directory or adding the location of the executable to your $PATH variable will do you no good if you do not own the file or the file does not have the execute bit set. However, if you do not have permission to execute the file or if the execution bit is not set, you will get a different error. In either of these cases, the error will say "Permission denied".

Redirecting Files and Output

The redirection of files and output can be achieved through the use of the following commands:

Redirection Commands		
Command	**Name**	**Description**
|	pipe	Make the output of the command to the left of the pipe the input to the command to the right of the pipe.
>		Send output to a new file or overwrite an existing file.
>>		Send output to a new file if the specified file does not exist. If the specified already exists, then append the output to the end of the file.
tee	tee	Send output to two places like standard output and a file simultaneously.

The following examples demonstrate the use of the redirection symbols.

#ls –al | grep x

The above command string sends the output of the ls –al command to the grep command. The grep command then displays only the lines of the ls – al output that contain the letter "x". The result is the listing only includes executable files or files with the letter x in the name.

#ls –al > file.out

The above command string sends the output of the ls –al command to the file named file.out. If the file.out did not exist before, it has just been created. If the file.out file did exist before, it has just been overwritten. In either case, the output is sent to the file only. No output is displayed on the screen.

#ls –al | tee file.out

The above command string sends the output of the ls –al command to the screen as well as to a file named file.out. If the file.out did not exist before, it has just been created. If the file.out file did exist before, it has just been overwritten. Notice that the tee command requires the help of the pipe when used in this manner. This is because tee is performing a command function rather than simply redirecting output.

Quoting Rules

The UNIX shell uses three characters for quoting: single quotes ('), double quotes ("), and backslashes (\). The following table explains the different methods of quoting and when to use them. Quotes allow characters to be used as literals. This allows the operating system to ignore special characters and words that would normally be commands.

Quoting Rules		
Type	**Description**	**When to Use Each Method of Quoting**
\	Backslash	A backslash (\) protects the next character except if it is a newline. (\n) If a backslash precedes a newline, it prevents the newline from being interpreted as a command separator.
' '	Single quotes	Single quotes ('...') protect everything (even backslashes, newlines, etc.) except single quotes, until the next single quote.
" "	Double quotes	Double quotes ("...") protect everything except double quotes, backslashes, dollar signs, and back quotes, until the next double quote. A backslash can be used to protect ", \, $, or ` within double quotes.

Exercises for UNIX Basics:

1. List all of the files in your current directory that have an "a" in the file name.

2. Send the output of a command to the end of an existing file without overwriting the file.

3. Who determines the standards for UNIX operating systems?

4. What is the "?" wildcard used for?

5. What are two advantages of using a thin client?

6. Use the man page to learn how to use the man page.

7. Display the active defined aliases.

8. Display the active environment variables.

9. Display just the value of the TERM environment variable.

10. What is a protocol?

2 WORKING WITH FILES

Copy

The *copy* [cp] command does just what the name implies. It makes an exact duplicate of the original file with whatever name you specify in your command syntax. The syntax of the copy command is cp [options] original_file new_file. While the contents of the new file will match that of the original file, the new file will be assigned its own inode. The *inode* is what the operating system uses to keep track of things like files. We'll discuss inodes in more detail later. For now you just need to know that the operating system uses inodes as unique identifiers for all files on the system.

The new file will inherit the default file permissions rather than that of the original file. If you need to be sure the new file possesses the same permissions and ownership as the original file, you will want to use the –p option. When used with the copy command, the –p option preserves the ownership and permissions of the original file for the new file.

You do not need to be working in the source or destination directory being referred to in your copy command syntax. However, if you are copying to or from a directory other than your current working directory, you will need to provide the absolute path for the files you are working with. If you need to copy an entire directory, including its contents and any possible sub-directories, you will need to use the –r option. The –r option makes a recursive copy from the starting point until the last file of the innermost nested sub-directory has been copied.

cp Command Options		
Command	**Option**	**Description**
cp		Make a copy of a file.
	-p	Preserving the ownership and permissions.
	-r	Recursive copy of a directory.

Occasionally, you may need to copy a file from one server to another. This task can be achieved with the *remote copy command* [rcp]. The use of this command will require some network configuration before it will work. Essentially, the two machines involved in the rcp syntax need to be aware of each other. This is accomplished by creating entries in the .rhosts and /etc/hosts.equiv files. These two files are used to provide trusted remote authentication. For specific directions, you should consult the man page for .rhosts, and hosts.equiv on your particular flavor of UNIX. The configuration of these files will also enable the use of the [rlogin] (remote login) and [rsh] (remote shell) commands. The syntax for the rcp command is (rcp original_file remote_hostname:new_file). After the hosts.equiv and .rhosts files have been configured correctly, the system should not ask you for a user name or password when executing an rcp command.

rcp Command Options		
Command	**Option**	**Description**
rcp		Make a copy of a file from a remote host.
	-p	Preserving the ownership and permissions.
	-r	Recursive copy of a directory.

For those environments that demand an extra level of security, UNIX offers the *secure copy* [scp] command. The scp command is very similar to the rcp command except it uses secure shell [ssh] for authentication. Before beginning the copy process, scp will ask for a password to access the remote server.

scp Command Options		
Command	Option	Description
scp		Make a secure copy of a file from a remote host.
	-C	Enable compression. This passes the –C flag to ssh.
	-p	Preserves original file attributes like mode, access time, and modification time.
	-P port #	Used to connect to a specific port on a remote host.
	-q	Turns off the default progress meter.
	-r	Recursive copy of a directory
	-v	Verbose mode. Causes scp and ssh to display progress messages. May be used for debugging.

Another form of copying a file is to make a link to it. A *soft* or *symbolic link* is essentially a virtual copy of a file in a new location. When you make a symbolic link to a file, what happens is instead of UNIX making a duplicate of the file, it simply creates a pointer to the original file.

There are a few differences between hard links and soft links. Perhaps the most significant one is that hard links cannot span filesystems and soft links can. Additionally, the first file created among hard links has the same status as those created after it. Unlike hard links, soft links, or symbolic links as they are frequently called, are all dependent on the original file.

If a file has been deleted but a process is holding it open, what you will temporarily end up with is an inode that has no links. The file will be removed from the inode table when the last process referencing the file completes.

If you use the ls command to list the contents of a directory that contains a symbolic link, you will see the file name listed with the rest of the files. It will seem like the file is local to that directory. But if you use the ls –l command to display a long listing of the directory contents, the first character on the left will display an "l" to identify that the file is actually a link. The rightmost column in the ls –l output will display the link file name, followed by an arrow that points to the right, followed by the original file's name. You must identify the original file by absolute path when creating a link if it is not in your current directory. If you do not, you will get an error saying that the original file does not exist. You will also get the same error if you get the filename and link name in the wrong order. The following examples illustrate the command syntax to make both hard and soft links:

#ln original_file link   (Creates a hard link)

ls -i /scripts/file1

   358979 /scripts/file1

ls -i /scripts/dir1/file1

   358979 /scripts/dir1/file1

The above output demonstrates that the original file /scripts/file1 and the hard link to that file located at /scripts/dir1/file1 are using the same inode to identify it. So although this file appears to exist in two places, as far as the operating system is concerned, there is just one file.

#ln –s original_file link   (Creates a soft link)

ls -i /scripts/file2

   358980 /scripts/file2

ls -i /scripts/dir1/file2

   413703 /scripts/dir1/file2

ls -al file2

   lrwxrwxrwx 1 root   root   14 Oct 23 15:52 file2 -> /scripts/file2

The above output demonstrates that the original file /scripts/file2 and the soft or symbolic link to that file located at /scripts/dir1/file2 are using unique inodes. So the operating system thinks of the original file and the soft link as separate files. However, if you look at the ls –al output, you can see that the soft link is clearly pointing to the original file, as indicated by the arrow on the right side of the output and the "l", which stands for link at the beginning of the output.

Moving or Renaming

The terms *move* and *rename* are used synonymously in the UNIX world. The truth is, there is no rename command. Both functions are accomplished with the move [mv] command. This is because to UNIX, moving a file from one location to another is the same as moving a file from one name to another. Remember, UNIX uses the file's inode to remember where it is. The names are just there for us people. You do not need to be sitting in the source or destination directory of the move command syntax in order to move a file between them. The command syntax to move a file within the same directory is (mv oldfile newfile). To move a file from your current directory to the /tmp directory, the syntax would be (mv oldfile /tmp/newfile). Actually, if the filename is going to be the same at the new location, you can save yourself some keystrokes and use the command syntax (mv oldfile /tmp/). The last slash at the end of /tmp/ tells UNIX to drop it in the /tmp directory with the same name.

Incidentally, it is always a good idea to use absolute paths if you are moving a file to a new directory so it ends up where you wanted it. If you miss place a file, you may be forced to learn how to use the [find] command. Actually, you should learn how to use the find command anyway, but it is better to learn how to use the find command before you HAVE to find something. That way you are more likely to be successful at finding it.

Removing or Deleting

The *remove* [rm] command is fairly self-explanatory. It is used to remove or delete unwanted files or directories. Be careful with this command. UNIX does not have a recycle bin. I really cannot stress this point enough. Once you remove a file, it is gone. If the file was created since the last backup was made of the system, there will be no way to get it back. The syntax for the remove command is simply the command followed by the file you want to remove (rm file). The remove command accompanied by the –r option is very efficient for recursively removing directories and everything in them. This includes sub-directories and anything in them as well. Because it is so efficient, it is also very dangerous. The operating system will not pause and ask you if you are sure. Once you hit the return key, whatever you told UNIX to remove will be gone. UNIX also offers the remove directory [rmdir] command. But the rmdir command only works on empty directories.

rm Command Options		
Command	**Option**	**Description**
rm		Remove a file.
	-r	Recursive remove a file or directory.

Listing, Finding, and Printing Files

The following section discusses how to find a file, how to generate lists of files, and how to tell what kind of file a file is. To accomplish these tasks, the [find], ls, [grep], [egrep], [fgrep], and [file] commands will be used. A brief discussion and example will be provided for each of these commands.

The Find Command

The *find command* does exactly what the name implies. It finds stuff. The find command has useful operands that can be coupled with it to help you find a file by the file's name, age, or size. My favorite way to use the find command is with the name operand because it allows wild cards to be used with it. This means that I do not have to know exactly what the file's name is to find it. Additionally, trying to find a file on a large system can take a while, so if you know what part of the system, or at least what filesystem, the file lives in, you can greatly cut down on the search time by telling find where to start looking. The syntax of how to find a file by name named testfile1 starting in the /tmp directory is as follows.

#find /tmp –name testfile1

The command line syntax breakdown for the preceding command line is demonstrated in the following manner:

Command	Where to Start Looking	Operand to Use	Name of the File
find	/tmp	-name	testfile1

The preceding example is pretty straightforward because it assumes that I know what the name of the file is and I know approximately where the file is located. If you do not remember exactly what I file is called but you remember part of the file's name, you can use a wild card. For example, let's say you remember that the file's name had "test" in it somewhere. We can use the asterisk "*" wildcard symbol before and after the word test to find all files with the word test somewhere in the name. A wildcard search function like this requires that the subject be enclosed in single tick marks like this: '*test*'. This tells the find command that the asterisks are not actually part of the file name but that they are wildcard symbols.

If we do not know where to look, we may have to run the command on a few directories or file systems before we find it. Alternately, if you have root or superuser permissions, you can start looking in the "/" root directory. This tells the find command to look everywhere in the system beginning in the root directory. The reason I do not recommend beginning in the root directory if you do not have root privileges is that your display will fill up with messages warning you that you do not have permission to look in a bunch of locations in the operating system. If you do have root privileges, then by all means go for it. You are not going to hurt anything by running a find command. So if we were to look for a file that had the word "test" somewhere in the name and we had no idea where to look and we had root privileges, the command syntax would look like the following:

#find / -name '*test*'

The command line syntax breakdown for the preceding command line is demonstrated in the following manner:

Command	Where to	Operand to	The File Has the Word

	Startlooking	Use.	"Test" in It
find	/	-name	'*test*'

The ls (List) Command

The *ls* or *list command* is perhaps the easiest-to-remember and most frequently used command. Type ls at any location in a UNIX operating system, and you will get a list of all visible files and directories contained in the current directory you are sitting in. To generate a similar list of a directory you are not sitting in, you either change to that directory first or just feed the ls command the absolute directory path as input. The ls command has plenty of options that can accompany it to show you various pieces of information or arrangements of the information. I typically always use the –a and the –l options. The –a is for all of the current directory's contents. Remember earlier I indicated that ls would show you all of the visible files and directories. If you use the –a option, you will also see the invisible contents. The invisible contents are any file or directory that has a dot or period as the first character. The –l option is for long output. I use this option to show me all of the information I will need related to the ownership, permissions, etc., of the subject I am looking at. Although the –a stands for all, I tell myself that –al together means all, because that way I can see all of the files and all of the information related to the files. That was the easiest way for me to remember it when I was getting started with UNIX. The remaining typically used and sometimes-useful command options for the ls command are included in the following table.

ls Command Options		
Command	**Options**	**Description**
ls		Lists the contents of a directory.
	-a	Displays all files including hidden files.
	-c	When used together with –lt displays files in modified time order.

	-g	Displays files in long format with group name but not the owner.
	-h	Display in human readable format.
	-l	Displays files in long format.
	-t	Displays files in create time order.

The GREP (Global Regular Expression Parser) Command

The *grep*, *egrep*, and *fgrep commands* can be used to locate a search argument in a file. The default output of the grep command is to display the entire line of the file that the search argument is located in. The grep command is very helpful when you are dealing with large files or commands that generate many pages of output. The grep commands are used as filters. They scan input and return only lines that contain the specified pattern as output omitting the rest. The grep command is actually an acronym for Global Regular Expression Parser or Print. The egrep version of the grep command uses full regular expressions that include the full alphanumeric and special character set. The fgrep is a Fast version of the grep command. It uses a different algorithm that searches for strings rather than a pattern.

grep Command Options		
Command	**Option**	**Description**
grep		Searches for lines that include a pattern.
	-c	Returns a count of the number of lines that contain a pattern.
	-i	Searches for lines that include a pattern in lower or uppercase form.
	-l	Returns on names of files that contain a pattern.
	-n	Precedes each line by its line number in a file.

	-v	Searches for lines that do not include a pattern.
	-w	Searches for lines that include a pattern as a separate word.

The file Command

The *file command* is used to discover what type of files you are looking at or working with. Unlike other operating systems, UNIX does not require different file types to include a file extension to identify what type of file it is. You may find that applications and users will use file extensions like txt or exe, but the extensions are for the convenience of humans only. The UNIX operating system does not need them. So when you need to know what type of file a file is, just use the file command. The syntax is simple. You can display the file types of all files in the local directory by typing "file *", or you can specify a specific file by name as follows: file filename. The following is an example of output from the file command issued in a directory that contains a tar file, a sub-directory, a text file, a zip file, and an executable script file.

#file *

coins.tar: USTAR tar archive

dir1:   directory

file1:   ascii text

stuff.zip: ZIP archive

test: commands text

The awk Programming Language

The *awk programming language,* or sometimes called the *awk line editor,* is used to format output and omit unnecessary information from command output. The following example directs input into awk with a pipe. It is then used to select the desired fields from the input and displays them on standard output. The second example shows the output without using awk to format the output. awk is mentioned in this section merely to note its usefulness as a tool to find and parse information. For more examples and command options, see the section that discusses awk in greater detail. The following two examples illustrate the difference of using grep to find a subject and using grep with awk to find a subject and weed out information you do not care to see.

#df –h | grep swap

swap   5.3G   48K   5.3G   1%   /var/run

swap   512M   768K   511M   1%   /tmp

#df –h | grep swap | awk '{print $4, $5, $6}'

5.3G 1% /var/run

511M 1% /tmp

Displaying and Printing Files

As with any other task in the UNIX operating system, there are multiple ways to display information from files, or files in their entirety. Some of the common commands to perform these tasks are the cat, pg, more, less, head, and tail commands. The following describes how the commands are used and how they differ from each other.

The *pg*, or *page command*, is used to display a file one page or one full screen at a time. The default behavior of the pg command is to display the first page of information and then pause until the enter key is hit. The file being displayed will then display the next page and pause again until the enter key is hit again and so on until the EOF is reached. The pg command will allow you to use the vi search function within the file if your EDITOR environment variable is set to vi. If you are finished viewing a file before the EOF is reached, you can use the Esc-c key sequence to return to the command prompt.

The *more command* will display the first page of a file similar to the pg command. The difference between the pg command and the more command is the more command will allow you to move through a file one line at a time or one page at a time. As with the pg command, the more command will advance one screen or page at a time by hitting the enter key. The more command also allows you to advance one line at a time by hitting the space bar. The vi search function may be used within the file. If you are finished viewing a file before the EOF is reached, you can use the Esc-c key sequence to return to the command prompt.

Similar to the more command is the less command. The *less command* will display the first page of a file, similar to the more command. The difference between the less command and the more command is the less command will allow you to move backward through a file at any point until the EOF is reached. The less command navigation functions for advancing one page at a time or one line at a time are the same as with the more command. The backward navigation is achieved with the use of the arrow keys. The less command will display a file faster than other commands because it does not read the entire file before displaying it on the screen. Depending on the speed of your UNIX server, this difference in performance may or may not be noticeable. The vi search function may be used within the file. If you are finished viewing a file before the EOF is reached, you can use the Esc-c key sequence to return to the command prompt.

The *cat* or *concatenate command* will display an entire file without pausing. The behavior of not pausing makes files difficult to read if they are longer than one page unless you use another command like pg in conjunction with it to add the pausing behavior. The cat command is very useful both at the command line and within scripts for finding a particular line or word if it is used in conjunction with one of the grep variants. The cat command can also be used to feed a file to a redirector like |, >, or <.

If you just want to display the beginning or the end of a file, the head and tail commands are the correct tool for the job. The default behavior of both the head and tail commands is to display 10 lines. You may alter the number of lines to display with the –n option. The syntax to change the number of lines is head –n filename. An important note is that you do not actually type the "n". The "n" is just a placeholder for the number of lines you want to view. So if you wanted to view 15 lines instead of the default 10, you would type head –15 filename.

Adding Line Numbers to Output

To add line numbers to command line output, you may use the [nl] or cat command with either the -n or –b option. The default behavior of the nl command is to insert line numbers at the beginning of each line in a file and display the file to standard output. The original file will not be modified. The line numbers will only be displayed on the screen. Similar to the nl command is the cat command when used with the –n or –b options. When the –n option is used with the cat command, it behaves as described previously in this chapter, except it also precedes each line with the line's appropriate line number. When the –b option is used with the cat command, it precedes each line that includes any sort of printed character with a line number. In other words, it does not display line numbers for blank lines. I tell myself that –b stands for no blanks or minus blanks because it gives me an association to remember the purpose of the option by. So if you need to know exactly how many lines are in a file, you will want to use the nl command or the cat –n command. If you do not need an exact number or you only need to know how many lines in a file contain text, the cat –b option will work for you.

Displaying a Banner

The *banner command* is basically used to grab the user's attention. A banner is typically used to broadcast the completion of a script, program, or something that requires user interaction. Whatever word or literal that follows the banner command when it is executed on the command line or in a script will be displayed on the screen with hash marks or pound signs six or seven characters high, depending on if the original letter was a lowercase letter or a capital letter. The banner command has options to modify the size and orientation of the output if you do not want to use the default size and orientation of the banner output. Use the man command to explore the banner command options further.

In order to better understand this output, observe the following example command line argument followed by the example output. As you can see, even though only the first letter in the banner argument is a capital letter, in the output, all of the letters are displayed in capital letter form. The difference is that in the banner output, the original capital letter is displayed one character taller than the rest of the word.

#banner Hello

```
#       #
#       # ###### #         #         ####
#       # # #        #         #        #   #
###### ###### #         #         #   #
#       # # #        #         #        #   #
#       # # #        #         #        #   #
#       # ###### ###### ###### ####
```

Displaying DOS Files in UNIX

Files that have been created or modified in a DOS or Windows environment will often include control characters, end of line markers, or carriage return symbols. Since these symbols are foreign to UNIX, the UNIX Kernel does not interprets the characters correctly and so may process the files or display them incorrectly. To deal with this situation, the [dos2unix] command was invented. The *dos2unix command* will strip out the unacceptable characters to make the file readable by UNIX correctly. So if you think a file is corrupt for some reason and you cannot figure out why, try using the dos2unix command to convert the file before giving up on it. The worst that can happen is the file will still be corrupt, so you have nothing to lose.

Conversely, a [unix2dos] command exists to insert the special characters into a file created or modified in a UNIX environment to allow the file to be processed, displayed, or printed properly in a DOS or Windows environment. If you send a text file to a Windows environment that was created with an editor on a UNIX system, the file will be readable. However, since there are no end of line markers or carriage return characters, a word-processing program in a Windows environment will usually display each paragraph as one long line. You can fix this by hitting the return key wherever the line should wrap on the screen in your word processor or convert the file with the unix2dos command on a UNIX system. The following two examples demonstrate the proper use of the dos2unix and unix2dos commands:

#dos2unix dosfile unixfile

#unix2dos unixfile dosfile

Printing Files

As with other operating systems, the way to print a file is to send a copy of the file to a print queue. The *print queue* is a holding area where print jobs wait their turn to be printed. In UNIX, a print queue must be configured for each printer the operating system is going to send print jobs to. The print job will sit in the print queue either until the operating system wakes up the printer and tells it there is a print job waiting in the queue or, if the printer is already active, the print job may sit in the print queue until the print jobs ahead of it in the queue are gone and the printer device is ready to process it. If there is only one print queue configured on the system, then that is the only printer the operating system knows about, and it will be the default printer for all print jobs. However, if there is more than one print queue configured, print jobs will need to be directed to a particular print queue with the [lp] command.

The [lp] command can be used to send a print job to a printer. If there is only one print queue defined, then the syntax is simply lp filename. However, if your operating system has multiple print queues defined, you will need to use the –d option to direct your print job to a particular printer. So if you want to send the print job to the printer you have named printer1, you would type the following syntax at the command prompt:

#lp –d printer1 printme (Where printme is the name of the file to be printed.)

To verify the print job went to the correct print queue, you may use the [lpstat] command, which will show you the current status of all defined print queues. The lpstat only shows what is currently waiting to be printed in the print queue. So if your print job prints before you can type the lpstat command, you will never see it listed in the queue. I usually use the lpstat command to monitor the status of print queues of very busy printers where users are frequently printing large batch reports. Sometimes a user will get anxious and submit the same print job multiple times because it did not print immediately. While the reason their print job did not print immediately may take some detective work, they will be calling you asking you to increase their priority in the print queue or to cancel the multiple print jobs they submitted that have finally begun to print over and over.

To modify the priority of a print job or to cancel it, run the lpstat command and note the print job-id. After you have the print job-id, you may use the lp –q job-id option to change the priority. The default print job priority is 50. The lowest print job priority setting is 1, and the highest print job priority is 100. You may cancel a print job with either the cancel or the lprm commands. The syntax of the cancel command is cancel job-id. Similarly, the syntax of the lprm command is lprm job-id.

To cancel a print job, use one of the following commands:

#cancel 101 (Where 101 is the job-id of the print job in the print queue.)

#lprm 101

To change the default print job priority, use one of the following commands.

#lp –q 1 101 (This sets the priority of print job-id 101 to the lowest possible priority.)

#lp –q 100 101 (This sets the priority of print job-id 101 to the highest possible priority.)

You may also use the cancel command to cancel all active print jobs submitted by a user or all print jobs in a print queue. The lpmove command can be used to move a print job between print queues. You may also do more fancy stuff with the lp command, like add a banner to the beginning of a print job, send the user a message when their print job is printed, or print on both sides of a piece of paper (provided your printer supports double-sided printing.). If you want to do this sort of fancy printing, I suggest you check out the man page for your operating system's version of the lp commands and verify that your network and printers can support the operations you want to perform, like two-sided printing and e-mail notifications.

lp Command Options		
Command	Option	Description
lp		Line print.
	-d	Identify destination for print job.
	-m	Sends an email when the print job is completed. This assumes mail is configured on the server.
	-q	Sets the priority of the print job.

Substituting or Removing Text from a File

The *[tr] command* can be used to translate characters in a file to another character. Unless otherwise directed, the output will be sent to standard output. This means that the characters will not actually be changed in the file by default, but the file will be displayed on your screen as if the file has changed. This is an important safety feature that allows you to view what the command syntax you have chosen will do before you actually commit to doing it to a file. To modify the contents of the file, you will need to redirect the output to a file. The following two examples demonstrate ways to direct input and output for the tr command. In the following example, file1 will be sent to standard output, but any occurrences of the letter k will be deleted. The contents of file1 will remain unaltered.

#tr –d k < file1

In the following example, file1 will be the input for the tr command. The –s flag will translate any occurrence of the lowercase k into an uppercase K. The output will be sent to file2. The contents of file1 will remain unaltered. If file2 already exists, it will be overwritten.

#tr –s k K < file1 > file2

If you truly wanted to change all occurrences of k to K in file1 at this point, all you would need to do is move file2 to file1. Although for the sake of your data, you should make a copy of file1 first. This is always a good idea when manipulating data because the end result is not always what you expect it to be. To replace the original file1 with the new modified version file2, use the following syntax:

#mv file2 file1

The following table defines the flags used with the tr command.

tr Command Options		
Command	Option	Description
tr		Translate a single character into another.
	-d	Delete the specified character.
	-s	Substitute a single character for another.

The following table contains examples of ways to manipulate strings in a file. These are just some quick examples to get you thinking. Obviously these methods can be combined, modified, and can incorporate other UNIX commands. You should play around with these scenarios until you understand what each part is doing and then develop your own method to suit your needs. Once you get good at this sort of thing, you can begin writing your own commands by writing a command string and then using the alias command to create a one-word name or command to execute the string. For example, you could write a string to change the case of letters and call the command "case". There are a few ways to do this in the following examples.

Manipulating Files Without Opening Them	
Command Syntax	Description
cat file1 | sed 's/abc/def/g' > file2	Replace the string abc with def. This command reads text from file1 and writes it to file2. Every occurrence of

	the string abc is replaced by def.
perl –i.bak -pe 's/abc/def/g' file1	Replace the string abc with def in the file itself, and generate a backup of the original file in file1.bak. This command reads text from the file file1 and writes it back into the same file where every occurrence of the string abc is replaced by def. The original contents of file1 are copied into file1.bak.
cat file1 | tr '[:upper:]' '[:lower:]' > file2	Change everything to lowercase. This command reads text from the file1 and writes it in lowercase to file2.
cat file1 | tr '[:lower:]' '[:upper:]' > file2	Change everything to uppercase. This command reads text from file1 and writes it in uppercase to file2.
cat file1 | tr '[a-z]' '[A-Z]' > file2	Change everything to uppercase. This command reads text from file1 and writes it in uppercase to file2.
cat file1 | tr -s '[:space:]' ' ' > file2	Replace whitespace with a single space. This command reads text from file1 and writes it to file2 after replacing all types of whitespace (horizontal and vertical) with a single space.
cat file1 | sed 's/[0-9]/ DIGIT /g' > file2	Replace digits with the string " DIGIT ". This command reads text from file1 and writes it to file2 after replacing all appearances of digits with the string " DIGIT ".
uniq file1 > file2	The *uniq command* is used to remove duplicate lines from being repeated immediately after each other in a file.

fold –w 10 file1 > file2	The *fold command* is used to wrap the lines in a file to a specified width. The *–w flag* is used to specify the desired width of the lines in the file.

Exercises for Working with Files:

1. Copy a file named file1 and name the copy file2.

2. Move a file named file2 to a file named file3 in the same directory.

3. Remove a file named file3.

4. Recursively remove all files and directories inside the /tmp directory.

5. List all of the files in the /var/tmp directory.

6. Direct the man page for the grep utility into a file called grep.out.

7. Display a listing of files in your home directory that do not have the number 1 in the name.

8. Make a copy of a file named file1 preserving its properties and name the file file4.

9. Display just the first 3 lines of a file named file1.

10. Display the lines of file1 that contain the letter (a) in them.

3 EDITORS

Using vi

"vi" stands for Visual Display Editor. It is pronounced like "vee eye," not like "vye" or "six". Either of the two preceding pronunciations will get you laughed at by UNIX users and Systems Administrators. Despite what you may have heard, vi is not that difficult to use. Don't be intimidated by all of the commands and shortcuts vi offers. I don't have them all memorized, and I use vi on almost a daily basis.

If I need to do a lot of repetitive editing, I just get my old cheat sheet out to remind myself about the most appropriate shortcut, and I'm off and editing. No big deal, right? So, let's get started. To start or enter the vi editor, type the letters "vi" followed by a file name. You may use an existing file name or a new one. To create a new file with vi, just start vi with a new file name and then save the file. If you do this and then exit vi, it will create an empty file with a size of 0 kilobytes.

You can use the ls –l command to verify that the file exists but is using no disk space. The system remembers about the file because it was assigned an inode when it was created. To use vi to edit an existing file, just enter vi and the name of the existing file at the command prompt and hit the return key. As long as you have write privileges on the existing file, you should have no trouble using vi to edit and then save the edits on the existing file.

Inodes (inodes)

Inodes or as the operating system knows them, "inodes" with a lowercase i, are data structures that contain information about files. Each file has an inode and is identified by an inode number. inodes keep track of information about files, such as user and group ownership, access mode (read, write, execute permissions), and type.

There are a set number of inodes per filesystem. If you run out of inodes, all you need is another filesystem. Realistically speaking, you should never run out of inodes, but it is theoretically possible. To run out of inodes, you would need to create a tremendous amount of files without ever removing any. Basically, you are more likely to run into other problems caused by lack of disk space or poor systems management before lack of available inodes becomes a problem. A file's inode number can be found using the ls –i command. For more detail about the file, you can add the –*l* flag.

Modes

vi has two modes used for two types of functions. The first mode is *command mode*. When you begin a vi session, it will automatically be in command mode. While in command mode, vi will accept basic cursor movement and file navigation instructions, perform pattern searches, and perform basic editing functions, like cut and paste or yank and put. The second mode is known by a few names, depending on whom you ask. You may hear *insert mode, edit mode,* or *input mode.* Whatever you choose to call the second mode, it is used to insert new and edit existing text in a file. For the purpose of discussion, I will refer to the second mode as edit mode. This makes the most sense to me since what we want to do in this mode is edit something. While in edit mode, you perform your actual editing of the file. To save your edits, you will need to first return to command mode. To return to command mode from edit mode, just hit the Esc or escape key to escape from edit mode. Whenever you are not sure which mode you are in, the safe thing to do is to go ahead and hit the escape key. If you were already in command mode, nothing happens. If you were in edit mode, you will be switched to command mode, at which point you can just go back to edit mode to make changes. Whenever I am trying to do something in vi and it is not working, the first thing I do is hit the escape key to make sure I am in the correct mode. If that does not fix the problem, I hit the Caps Lock key. Since the vi edit mode shortcut keys are case sensitive, if you accidentally hit the Caps Lock key while you are typing, the shortcut keys will stop working.

Moving the Cursor

To move the cursor, put vi in command mode and use the following commands.

Command Mode Cursor Navigation (shortcuts)	
Command	**Description**
h	One space to the left.
k	One line up.
j	One line down.
l	One space to the right.
(Return)	Beginning of new line.
-	Beginning of previous line.
^	Beginning of current line.
$	End of current line.
w	Beginning of next word.
b	Beginning of current word.
c	End of current word.
Ctrl-e	Scroll forward (type "e" while holding down the Ctrl key.).
Ctrl-b	Scroll backward (type the "b" while holding down the Ctrl key.).
G	Move to the end of the file.

:set number	Display line numbers in the vi session for the file.
.exrc file	Creating this file in your home directory will automatically turn on line numbers for all of your vi editing sessions.
/pattern/	Search for the specified pattern.
n	Next occurrence in file following a pattern search.
N	Previous occurrence in file following a pattern search.

The following commands may be used to make edits to a file while in command mode.

Command Mode Editing Commands (Shortcuts)	
Command	**Description**
:#co#	Insert a copy of the line number identified by the first number after the line number identified by the second number.
dd	Delete the current line.
dw	Delete the current word the cursor is resting on.
#dd	Delete the specified number of lines.
p	Put – Insert whatever is in the edit buffer from a delete or yank command.
u	Undo the last edit. (Does not work if the file has been saved since the last edit.)
U	Undo the edits made to the current line.
x	Delete the current character the cursor is resting on.
X	Delete the character to the left of the current location of

	the cursor.
r[x]	Replace the character where the cursor is with the [x] character.
yy	Yank – remove the current line and place it in the edit buffer.
#yy	Yank the specified number of lines.

The following vi commands may be used to enter edit mode from command mode with different editing actions.

Commands to Enter Edit Mode	
Command	**Description**
a	Appends text to the right of the cursor.
i	Inserts text to the left of the cursor.
o	Opens a new line below the line where the cursor is.
O	Opens a line above the location where the cursor is.

To quit or exit the current vi session, use the Esc key to get to command mode, and then use one of the following key sequences, depending on what you are trying to do. Occasionally, I get interrupted by a co-worker or a telephone call while editing a configuration file. When something like this happens, unless I have a lot of time invested in the current edit session since the last save, I will usually use :q! to quit my session without saving and then start over. This is usually safer than making a mistake with a configuration file because I forgot what I was doing. It can also be less time-consuming than figuring out where I lost my place.

One of the things that ticks me off about vi is that it will let me edit a file that does not have the write bit set. Or at least it appears to let you until you try to save the file. It will then give you a rude message indicating that you cannot save the file. If you are the owner of the file or the root user, you can use :w! to force the write of the file. Make sure you know what you are doing if you do this. Usually the permissions are set a certain way for a good reason. If you do not own the file, then you just wasted your time and you'll have to go find the System Administrator to do it for you or grant you write permissions on the file.

vi Editor Commands	
Command	**Description**
:w [filename]	Writes changes to [filename].
:q	Quits vi after above sequence is given.
:q!	Quits without any changes to the file being edited.
ZZ	Writes file and quits.

Saving Time at the Command Line

Recalling previously typed commands at the command prompt.

Two methods can be used to set up the recall feature in the UNIX shell environment. The first method is to include the line set -o vi in your .profile file. This takes precedence over variables that may have been set up for all users. The second method is to set the EDITOR environment variable to vi.

Editing the command line so that you don't have to retype it.

Once the recall feature has been set up, the Esc-k key sequence (type the Esc escape key and the letter k key at the same time) will recall previously used commands to the command line. Using the Esc-k sequence will retrieve the last command you executed on the command line. Continuing to hit the k key will scroll through your previously entered commands. A command will not be executed until you press the enter key. If you cannot find what you are looking for, you can use the Ctrl-c key sequence to return to the command prompt without executing any commands.

To save time and keystrokes at the command line, you can recall previously used commands and edit them if need be with vi editing commands. You may set how many commands will be retrievable with the Esc-k recall with the HISTORY environment variable. The HISTORY environment variable has a default setting that may vary depending on the flavor of UNIX you are using. Use the env command to display your shell environment variables to see what your HISTORY environment variable is set to. Once you know what it is set to, you can change it if you think the default setting will not meet your needs.

Introduction to awk

The *[awk] command,* or more correctly stated, programming language, is a very powerful tool frequently used to clean up, parse, and rearrange the text or numerical output from other UNIX commands. Before we get into awk, I would like to clear up a few common misconceptions about awk and perhaps provide some trivia for the next gathering of Geeks you attend. The sed and awk tools are often mentioned together as if they are one tool. I have seen books with sed and awk together in the title. Perhaps this is simply because there is not enough interesting material available to write an entire book on one or the other subject, so they are combined into one source. Whatever the reason, my point is that although they can certainly be used in conjunction with one another, sed and awk are not dependent on each other. They are separate tools that were developed separately.

Now for the trivia. The name awk does not actually mean anything like some UNIX commands that are abbreviations for proper English words. The letters a, w, and k are actually the first letters of the last names of the developers that created awk. The names of the three developers are Alfred Aho, Peter Weinberger, and Brian Kemighan. These three gentlemen worked together at Bell labs in the 1970s when they developed awk.

Since the development of the original awk, there have been other releases developed. The other releases are [gawk], which is the GNU version of awk; [mawk], which is a speedier rewrite of awk; and [nawk], which is the new version of awk. I am going to focus on the original awk because it has been around the longest and will be included in whatever version of UNIX you are using. Suffice it to say that these are all simply updated versions of awk that were developed with the idea of adding improvements. That being said, the topics covered for awk will also apply to the newer versions of awk.

The vi, sed, and awk tools are all essentially used to manipulate text. Since I have included material for vi, sed, and awk, I believe it makes sense to take a moment to offer a recommendation on what situation calls for what tool. You do not have to learn all three of these tools, but if you do, you will wonder how you did things before you mastered the three tools. The vi tool should be used to perform selective file manipulation. The sed tool should be used to perform simple repetitive tasks, like global character substitution or deletion. The awk tool should be used for more complex tasks, like formatting, rearranging, and omitting columns of data from the output of a UNIX command or from an existing file.

The following table includes some command options that you may wish to learn for data manipulation that is more detailed than moving columns of output.

awk Command Options		
Command	Option	Description
awk		
	d	Delete
	g	Globally replace the pattern space by the hold space.
	n	Don't print this line unless directed to with the p option.
	p	Override the n option.
	s	Substitute the first occurrence on a line.

Things that awk is not really well suited for are large or complicated tasks. Since awk is an interpreted language, awk scripts require the binary to run them. This means basically that you cannot compile the awk script and then run it by itself on a system that does not include the awk binary program. Compared to compiled code, awk scripts run relatively slowly because every time an awk script is run, the script is interpreted by the awk binary that is called by the operating system. However, as I said, the difference between compiled codes and interpreted script is vast in computer processing time, but to a human, the difference is negligible. You probably will not even notice that the script is being read. Most of the time, the response to an executed awk script should seem instant at the command prompt. If the processing time difference is a problem for you, than you can purchase a second party compiler application to compile and speed up the processing time, but you will have to pay for such a program where awk comes with the UNIX operating system at no additional charge.

Although the tasks I use awk for the most frequently are quick and dirty juggling of data, awk can actually be used for more sophisticated tasks, like creating small databases and performing mathematical operations on files that contain numerical data. The mechanisms that awk uses to perform functions are simple enough that people familiar with programming languages like BASIC or C should pick it up with no problem. If you have never worked with a programming language before, simply observe the following one liner examples to figure out what individual functions awk can perform, then move on to more complicated functions addressed by the database section. You will have it figured out in no time.

Command Line Examples (One Liners)

It is easy to use awk from the command line to perform simple operations on text files. Suppose I have a file named "coins" that describes a coin collection. Each line in the file contains the following information: the mineral the coin is made of; the weight of the coin measured in ounces, the date the coin was minted, the country of origin, and a description of the coin.

Sample File for the Following awk Examples				
Mineral	**Weight in Oz**	**Date**	**Country**	**Description**
gold	1	1986	USA	American Eagle
silver	10	1981	USA	Ingot
gold	1	1984	Switzerland	Ingot
gold	1	1979	RSA	Krugerrand
gold	0.1	1986	PRC	Panda
silver	1	1986	USA	Liberty One Dollar Piece
gold	0.25	1986	USA	Liberty Five Dollar Piece
gold	0.25	1987	USA	Constitution Five Dollar Piece
gold	1	1988	Canada	Maple Leaf

To invoke awk to list all the gold pieces as follows:

#awk '/gold/' coins

The preceding syntax tells awk to search through the file for lines of text that contain the string "gold", and print them out. The result is:

```
gold   1    1986  USA          American Eagle

gold   1    1984  Switzerland  Ingot

gold   1    1979  RSA          Krugerrand
```

gold	0.1	1986	PRC	Panda
gold	0.25	1986	USA	Liberty Five Dollar Piece
gold	0.25	1987	USA	Constitution Five Dollar Piece
gold	1	1988	Canada	Maple Leaf

This sort of searching through a file for content is easily enough accomplished with other UNIX commands like grep or find, so you may ask yourself why should you learn how to use awk. While it is true that grep and find are capable of finding the gold coins in the file, awk is capable of doing so much more than just finding a target and displaying what it finds. For example, suppose I am not interested in all of the information in the coins file and just want to know the descriptions of the coins. With awk I can easily omit the information I do not want. To accomplish this, all I have to do is rerun the previous awk syntax and add the numerical variable for the columns I want to print. In this case, I know that the description field contains from one to four pieces of data (words) and begins in the fifth column of the file. Remember for those lines in the file that have just a one- or two-word description, awk will just ignore the missing columns or print them as blank. Either way, it will look the same to you. So I would modify the previous syntax to include columns 5 thru 8 as follows:

```
#awk '/gold/ {print $5, $6, $7, $8}' coins
```

The new output would then be as follows:

American Eagle

Ingot

Krugerrand

Panda

Liberty Five Dollar Piece

Constitution Five Dollar Piece

Maple Leaf

The following example demonstrates the simplest form of syntax in an awk script:

#awk <search pattern> {<program actions>} filename

The awk binary searches through the input file for each line that contains the search pattern. For each line found that meets the search criteria, awk then performs the specified actions. In this example, the action is specified as {print $5, $6, $7, $8}, so awk prints the fifth through the eighth column of data which in the coins file is the description. The purpose of the print statement is to display column five through eight only. The preceding $ with the numerical column identifier identifies it as a field variable, which stores the words in each line of text by their numeric sequence. $1, for example, stores the first word in the line, $2 has the second, and so on. By default, a *word* is defined as any string of printing characters separated by spaces.

Since coins has the structure of mineral, weight in oz, date, country, and description, then the field variables are matched to each line of text in the file as follows:

mineral: $1

weight: $2

date: $3

country: $4

description: $5 through $8

The program action in this example prints the fields that contain the description. The description field in the file may actually include from one to four words, but that's not a problem, since "print" simply ignores any undefined fields. Awk's default program's logical action is to print the entire line, which is what print does when invoked without parameters. This means that the first example:

#awk '/gold/' coins, is the same as #awk '/gold/ {print}' coins

Note that awk recognizes the field variable $0 as representing the entire line, so this could also be written as:

#awk '/gold/ {print $0}' coins

The following example evaluates the variable in column 3 and displays the Date and Description for coins minted after 1986. The example adds some new concepts. No search pattern is specified in order to include all lines of data, which is awk's default behavior. Therefore, the formatting actions specified will be applied to all lines of data.

#awk '{if ($3 > 1986) print $3, "   ",$5,$6,$7,$8}' coins

The resulting output is as follows:

1987 Constitution Five Dollar Piece

1988 Maple Leaf

To add text or spaces to output lines, simply add them to the print statement (in this case, I added four spaces) by enclosing them in quotes. The default separation between columns separated with the comma is one space. I made the four spaces one literal word and added it to the parameter list. I like to separate columns of data for readability, but the important lesson to take away from this is that you have options on how the output from your commands and scripts will be displayed. You will find that once you have mastered the basics of awk, it is much easier to manipulate data at the command line than it is to copy and paste it into a spreadsheet program to rearrange the columns. Believe me, I have seen this done more than once and all I can do is walk away and shake my head.

An if statement is used to check the value of the date field for a number greater than 1986. If a value greater than 1986 is found, the print statement is executed. If the value of the date field is equal to or less than 1986, nothing happens. The awk statement will simply move on and evaluate the next line in the file.

Unlike most computer languages, awk makes no distinction between strings of alphabetic data and numbers. All the fields are regarded as strings, but if a string also happens to represent a number, numeric operations can be performed on the string. So we can perform an arithmetic comparison on the date field.

The next example prints out the number of coins in the collection. More precisely, the logic determines how many lines or records are in the file.

#awk 'END {print NR,"coins"}' coins

The result of this one line awk script is: 9 coins.

The first new item in this example is the END statement. To explain this, I have to extend the general form of an awk program to:

#awk 'BEGIN   {<initializations>}

    <search pattern 1> {<program actions>}

    <search pattern 2> {<program actions>}

    END   {<final actions>}'

The BEGIN clause performs any initializations required before awk starts scanning the input file. The subsequent body of the awk program consists of a series of search patterns, each with its own program action. The awk program scans each line of the input file for each search pattern, and performs the appropriate actions for each string found. Once the file has been scanned, an END clause can be used to perform any final actions required.

So, since all this example does is count the number of records in the file, the example doesn't perform any processing on the input lines. All the example does is scan through the file and perform a final action: print the number of lines in the file, which is provided by the NR variable. The variable NR stands for "number of records". NR is one of awk's pre-defined variables. There are others; for example, the variable NF gives the number of fields in a line.

If the current price of gold is $475 per ounce, and I want to figure out the approximate total value of the gold pieces in the coin collection, I can execute the awk script as follows:

#awk '/gold/ {ounces += $2} END {print "value = $" 475*ounces}' coins

The result of this one line awk script is: value = $2185

In this example, ounces is a user-defined variable. You can use almost any string of characters as a variable name in awk, as long as the name doesn't conflict with some string that has a specific meaning to awk, such as print or NF. A variable handled as a string variable is initialized to the null string, so there is no need to manually set the value to null. Similarly, a numeric variable will be initialized to zero. So the program action to set column two of the coins file to ounces is as follows:

{ounces += $2}

The preceding line sums the weight of the coin on each matched line of the coins file into the variable ounces. The += operator is a shorthand way of expressing:

{ounces = ounces + $2}

The next and final action in this awk script is to compute and print the value of the gold coins in the coins file with the following syntax:

END {print "value = $" 475*ounces}

The only thing here of interest is that the two print parameters, the literal '"value = $"' and the expression "475*ounces", are separated by a space, not a comma. This concatenates the two parameters together on output, without any spaces between the dollar sign and the numerical value of the coins.

Program Example (Including Logic from the One Liner Examples)

Each of the preceding one liner examples displays a piece of program logic for displaying information from the coins file. However, if awk is used as a program instead of at the command line, it can extract all of the information at once. The following shows how to execute all of the one liner command line logic in a single program with awk.

#awk -f <awk program file name>

The following summary report is one possible output format solution for an awk program for the coins file:

Coin Collection Summary Report:

Gold pieces: nn

Weight of gold pieces: nn.nn

Value of gold pieces: n,nnn.nn

Silver pieces: nn

Weight of silver pieces: nn.nn

Value of silver pieces: n,nnn.nn

Total number of pieces: nn

Value of collection: n,nnn.nn

The following awk program generates this information:

```
# This is an awk program that summarizes a coin collection.

/gold/   { num_gold++; wt_gold += $2 }     # Weight of gold.

/silver/ { num_silver++; wt_silver += $2 }  # Weight of silver.

END { val_gold = 475 * wt_gold;            # Compute value of gold.

    val_silver = 15 * wt_silver;            # Compute value of silver.

    total = val_gold + val_silver;

    print "Coin Collection Summary Report:"; # Print report header.

    printf ("\n");

    printf ("  Gold pieces:              %2d\n", num_gold);

    printf ("  Weight of gold pieces:    %5.2f\n", wt_gold);

    printf ("  Value of gold pieces:     %7.2f\n",val_gold);
```

71

```
printf ("\n");

printf ("    Silver pieces:                    %2d\n", num_silver);

printf ("    Weight of silver pieces:      %5.2f\n", wt_silver);

printf ("    Value of silver pieces:       %7.2f\n",val_silver);

printf ("\n");

printf ("    Total number of pieces:      %2d\n", NR);

printf ("    Value of collection:      %7.2f\n", total); }
```

As with any UNIX file, comments can be inserted in the program by preceding them with a #. Note the statements num_gold++ and num_silver++ use the ++ operation to increment the identified variables by one. Multiple statements can be written on the same line by separating them with a semicolon (;). The semicolon is the end-of-line character. So the awk binary just treats what is after the semicolon as if it is on the next line of the program. Note the use of the printf statement, which offers more flexible printing capabilities than the regular print statement. The general syntax of a printf statement is as follows:

```
printf("<format_code>",<parameters>)
```

There is a format code for each of the parameters in the list. Each format code determines how its corresponding parameter will be formatted on the printed report. The format code %2d tells awk to print a two-digit number, and the format code %7.2f tells awk to print a seven-digit floating-point number, with two digits to the right of the decimal point. Each string printed by printf in the example program ends with a \n, which is an ASCII code for a new line. Unlike the print statement, which advances the output to the next line by default when it prints a line, printf does not. The default behavior of printf is to append its output to the same line. A newline code forces the output to skip to the next line.

I saved this program in a file named coins.scr, and executed it as follows:

```
#awk -f coins.scr coins
```

The result of the summary output is as follows:

Coin Collection Summary Report:

Gold pieces:	7
Weight of gold pieces:	4.60
Value of gold pieces:	2185.00
Silver pieces:	2
Weight of silver pieces:	11.00
Value of silver pieces:	176.00
Total number of pieces:	9
Value of collection:	2361.00

Using sed

The *[sed] command* is a program for editing data. It stands for stream editor. The general syntax of the sed command is (sed command options input file). The sed command options will be applied to each line of the input file. If no input file is specified, then standard input is assumed. As sed applies the indicated command options to each line of input, it writes the results to standard output unless otherwise directed. I almost always direct sed to send its output to an output file. If you do not do this, you will have to rerun the same sed command syntax every time you want to reference the edited data. If you're going to use the cpu cycles to edit a stream of data, you may as well put them somewhere you can use them in the future. The exception here is if you know you will just need to see the edited data once or if you want to see that you got the sed syntax correct before saving it. The following table has the typical command options used for making simple stream editing.

sed Command Options		
Command	Option	Description
sed		
	d	Delete.
	g	Replace the contents of the pattern space with the contents of the hold space.
	-n	Don't print this line unless directed to with the p option.
	p	Print (Override the n option).
	s	Substitution.

d - Delete

This option is pretty straightforward. So be careful with it. The danger comes from its simplicity. The d option will delete whatever you tell it to, not whatever you meant to tell it to. A good practice is to send the output for a delete function to the screen so you can review it before you commit to saving the output to a file. The following sed command syntax demonstrates how to delete lines that contain the word "junk" from a file.

#sed '/junk/d' < filename

The preceding syntax demonstrates how to just get rid of an entire line since the function of the d option is to delete the target of the matched expression. If you want to remove the matched expression and replace it with something else, you will want to use the s option. The s option substitutes a specified value when the search expression is matched.

g - Global

Like most UNIX utilities, the default behavior of sed is to work on files, reading one line at a time. If you tell sed to change a word, it will only change the first occurrence of the word on a line. If you want to make the same change to all occurrences of an expression on every line in the file, you will need to use the "g" global option. To create a functional example with the global option included, execute the sed command with any input file as follows to globally replace the lowercase letter "a" with the uppercase letter "A". Since we are just sending the output to the screen, no output file will be created and the original file will not be modified, so you can use any file you have read access to.

#sed 's/a/A/g' < filename

-n – No Printing

By default, sed prints every line to standard output. Any substitutions that are made are printed to standard output instead of the original text of a file. If you use the optional "-n" argument in a sed statement, sed will not print the new lines. The following line will not print any output to standard output, but the changes will be sent to the output file.

#sed -n 's/pattern/&/' < filename > filename.out

p – Print

By default, sed prints every line to standard output. Any substitutions that are made are printed to standard output instead of the original text of a file. If you use the optional "-n" argument in a sed statement, sed will not print the new lines. When the "-n" option is used, the "p" option will cause the modified line to be printed

#sed -n 's/pattern/&/p' < filename

s - Substitution

sed is used for multiple editing functions, but perhaps the most common is the function of substitution. That is, sed can substitute a specific occurrence of a target or all occurrences of a target to something else. The substitute command option is the lower case "s". A simple example would be to change every occurrence of the word "Sunday" in a calendar file to the word "Funday". To perform this action, you would execute the following sed statement:

#sed s/Sun/Fun/ < calendar > calendar.new

I didn't put quotes around the argument because this example didn't need them. If your target includes special characters that sed or UNIX might misinterpret, like $, %, or #, the safe thing is to use quotes. The quotes tell whatever application you are using, sed in this case, to treat the special character as a literal with no special properties. Using quotes when they are not required does not hurt anything, so it is a good habit to get into since you are just starting. To use quotes with the previous statement, put the opening quote before the substitution s and the closing quote following the final slash / like this:

#sed 's/Sun/Fun/' < calendar > calendar.new

There are four pieces to the above sed substitute command. The first part is the single s before the first slash. The single s indicates that you are performing a substation function. The second part is the slash / delimiters. The slashes are used to separate the parts of the sed command. The third piece is the word "Sun". In this command, Sun is the regular expression pattern string. In other words, it is the thing that you want to get rid of and replace with something else. The fourth piece of this command is the word "Fun". In this command, Fun is the replacement string. In other words, you want to replace the value of the regular expression pattern string with the value of this word. So with the explanation of substitution, quoting, delimiters, and expressions, you have what you need to perform most of the tasks sed is regularly used for.

Substitute Flags

You can add additional functionality to a substitute command string by tacking on an additional option flag following the final delimiter. Such a flag can be used to specify what happens when there is more than one occurrence of an expression on a single line, and what to do if a substitution is found.

The Delimiter

The character after the s is the delimiter. By convention, it is normally a forward slash "/". This is primarily because other UNIX utilities like the ed editor and the vi editor use the slash also. However, you can use anything you want for the delimiter. The only time I have trouble with the slash character is when dealing with paths in a expression. In this case, if you choose to use the slash as your delimiter, you will need to precede any slash with a back slash. Doing so tells sed to ignore the following slash. The following example shows an example of this type of hard-to-read syntax:

#sed 's/\/home\/joe/\/home\/jon/' < filename > filename.new

Perhaps the simplest way to avoid this type of confusion is to use another character for the delimiter when there is a slash contained in the expression. To do this, just replace the delimiter with another character, like a comma, and leave the slashes in the expression. The following example is the same logical sed statement with commas used for the delimiters.

#sed 's,/home/joe,/home/jon,' < filename > filename.new

Using & as the Matched Expression String

Sometimes you will want to search for a pattern and add some characters, like parentheses or braces, around a pattern you found. This is easily accomplished if you know exactly what you are looking for. However, if you are not sure exactly what every occurrence in a file will be, you will need to use the special character ampersand "&". The way to use the ampersand solution is to add the "&" character in the place of the regular expression replacement string. This tells sed to replace whatever it finds with the same thing plus the characters you wanted to add, like parentheses or braces. The following example is not very practical, but it will be very obvious what has happened to the output, and that is what we want. The following sed statement should place parentheses around all lowercase letters in a file. Again, you may use any file for this demonstration because we are just sending output to the screen. We are not actually modifying a file.

#sed 's/[a-z]/(&)/g' < filename

The following table includes syntax examples for using the sed options listed in the previous table. Although these types of edits may seem basic, learning how to perform these types of edits with a stream editor like sed will save you a tremendous amount of time that would have been spent performing the same edits manually with an editor like vi.

Useful sed Syntax Examples	
Command	**Description**
sed '5d' < file	Delete line 5 of a file.
sed '/fish/d' file	Delete lines that contain the string fish.
sed '/[Tt]est/d' < file	Delete all lines containing Test or test.
sed –n '20,25p' file	Print only lines 20 through 25 from file.
sed '1,10s/fish/Better/g' file	Change fish to Better wherever it appears in the first 10 lines of file.
sed '/jan/s/-1/-5/' file	Change the first –1 to –5 on all lines containing jan.
sed 's/...//' file	Delete the first three characters from each line of file that contains text.
sed `s/...$//` file	Delete the last three characters from each line of file that contains text.

Combining Multiple sed Commands

Occasionally you may want to string together multiple sed commands. One way to accomplish this is to use the "-e" option before each command. It is not necessary to use the "-e" option with the previous examples because sed knows what to do when you only execute one edit command at a time. However, if you are going to execute multiple sed edits in a continuous string, you will need to let the sed editor know what is coming so it understands. If you fail to do so, you will get a response that says something to the effect of "#sed: command garbled". The following syntax demonstrates the proper use of the "-e" option with two sed commands in a row:

#sed -e 's/abc/ABC/' -e 's/xyz/XYZ/' –e 's/123/ABC/'< filename

If you tried this out on a test file that had multiple occurrences of abc or xyz on any single line, only the first occurrences were substituted. This is because the example syntax did not include the g option to make the edit globally. Remember, if you do not use the g option, you are only making the edit on the first occurrence of the matched search expression for each line of the input file.

If you want to do this, but you do not like the way it looks on the command line, you can use the "\" backslash character to break up the lines. This is handy if you are putting multiple sed commands together in a script. You will find it much easier to read. The following example demonstrates how to perform the same edits as the previous example but with the syntax separated into two lines. The same logic applies for multiple edits spread over multiple lines.

```
# sed -e 's/abc/ABC/' \
-e 's/xyz/XYZ/' \
-e 's/123/ABC/' < filename
```

Specifying a Number of Occurrences

With no flags, the first pattern is changed. With the "g" option, all patterns are changed. If you want to modify a particular pattern that is not the first one on the line, you can add a number after the substitution command to indicate you only want to match that particular pattern. Sound confusing? It really isn't. Just check out the following examples:

```
#sed 's/abc/ABC/2' < filename
```

```
#sed 's/abc/ABC/20' < filename
```

You may never need to just edit the 20th occurrence of something, but if you do, you'll be ready. Ha! But honestly, if you deal with large files of numbers or repetitive data, this will come in handy. You are lucky if you are just now starting to use sed. In the early days of sed, we could only edit occurrences of the first nine matches of any particular search pattern because there was a bug with sed that caused a problem with searching for occurrences stated with double digits. So if you are having problems with a double-digit occurrence edit, ask your system administrator nicely to update the sed binary in your system. However, realistically speaking, some other system requirement or security bulletin should have required a newer version of binaries long before you make your request.

Restricting sed by Line Number

Restricting sed edits to a specific line number is easy. You just insert the line number after the first tick mark and before the edit option. In the following syntax example, I want to perform a substitution only on the third line of the input file.

#sed '3 s/abc/ABC/' < filename

Restricting sed to Ranges of Lines

Restricting sed edits to a range of lines within a file is almost as easy as restricting sed edits to a specific line number. The difference is that you have to identify the first and last numbers of the range and separate them with a comma. In the following syntax example, I want to perform a substitution only on the lines within the range of line three through line thirty of the input file.

#sed '3,30 s/abc/ABC/' < filename

Combining sed with Other UNIX Programs

Similar to other UNIX utilities, part of the flexibility of sed stems from how easy it is to combine sed syntax with another UNIX command to perform a more powerful function than either utility is capable of individually. When I say combine, I mean to use in conjunction with. Don't waste your time trying to actually rewrite the binaries to perform functions they were not originally intended for. To combine sed with another UNIX command, just use the pipe "|" to feed the sed output to another UNIX command as input. You may also use the pipe to feed sed input from the output of other UNIX commands. The following table includes examples of sed being used at the beginning, in the middle, and at the end of various combinations of combined UNIX commands. Check out the examples and then come up with a few of your own and try them out. The coins file refers to the file used in the awk section.

| sed Combined With Other UNIX Commands ||
Command	Description
sed 's/^g.*//' coins | grep -v '^$' | wc -l	Count lines in the coins file that do not start with a (g).
cat coins | sed 's/gold/mold/g' | awk '/old/' | awk '{print $1, $2, $3}'	Change (gold) to (mold) and print fields 1, 2, and 3 from lines in the coins file that contain (old).
cat file1 | sed –F, '/abc/d' | awk '{print $2; print $1}'	Delete lines that contain (abc) and print columns 2 and 1 on their own line with a comma as a field delimiter.

Using sed in a Program

The previous sed examples can be used either at the command line or from within a script or a program. If you want to write a program to make changes in a file, sed is the tool to use. There are a few programs in the UNIX users or administrator's toolset that really help you get the job done. Be sure to learn and take advantage of them. The sed editor is definitely one of the UNIX tools you should learn. How proficient you choose to become with using sed depends on you and the type of work you are going to use it for.

sed -f scriptname

If you want to make a large number of edits with sed on a file, you can put all of the edits you want to make in a single file. You then just save the file and keep it updated if you are going to make the same edits in the future or if you want to make the same edits and new requirements may come up in the future. The following is the contents of a simple file called "sededits" that contains three separate edits I want to make on an input file. Keep in mind that I could have added much more than three edits to the file.

s/cow/calf/g

s/monkey/Monkey/g

s/puppy/dog/g

   Notice that each line of the file does not include the call to the sed editor (it does not include the word sed.). nor does it include the input file. All the entries in the sededits file needs is the actual command functions that we want the sed editor to take care of. So now that we have our sededits file ready, we can use the "-f" option to identify the sededits file as a file that contains sed commands. By doing so, we are telling sed what to do with the file. It knows to read the file and interpret the file contents as sed commands. Then we just feed it an input file like normal as demonstrated in the following syntax:

#sed -f sededits < filename

Exercises for Editors

1. What two modes are available with the vi editor?

2. How can you delete the line the cursor is sitting on in vi?

3. How can you delete the character the cursor is sitting on in vi?

4. What key sequence is used to exit a vi editing session without saving any changes?

5. What is the option used to perform a substitute function with sed?

6. What is the option used to perform a delete function with sed?

7. How do you make a sed function occur on every instance of a search argument?

8. What is the environment variable used to define the editor used at the UNIX command line?

9. How do you set up the recall function to redisplay previously typed commands?

10. What key sequence is used to recall a previously typed command?

4 FILESYSTEMS, DIRECTORIES, AND PATHS

The UNIX operating system has a hierarchical structure. The filesystems and directory structure can be represented with an inverted tree diagram. Just as a tree has roots, the operating system has a root directory from which all other directories stem.

The root directory is represented by the forward slash symbol /. At boot time the operating system reads the filesystem configuration file being used by your particular flavor of UNIX. Some locations you may find the filesystem configuration file are /etc/vfstab, /etc/filesystems, or /etc/fstab. For the purposes of this discussion, I will refer to vfstab as the configuration file being used. The vfstab provides the operating system kernel instructions on what order to mount the filesystems and where to mount them. When I say "mount", that refers to the location the filesystem will be found in the tree diagram for your system. Every filesystem has a mount point.

The *mount point* is the directory which is the absolute path where the filesystem starts. The mount point is one of the pieces of information stored in the vfstab. The vfstab also includes information like what storage device a filesystem is associated with, what type of filesystem each filesystem is, and if a filesystem should be automatically mounted at boot time. The vfstab is stored in the /etc directory. Since /etc is not a filesystem, it is a subdirectory of the root directory (/). So it is located in the root filesystem.

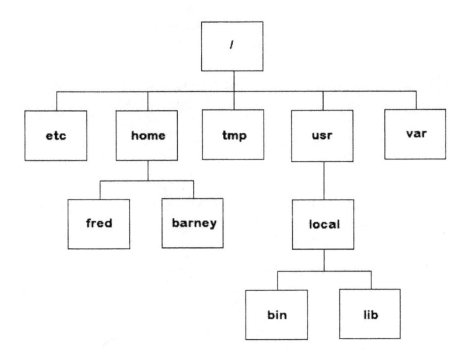

A path in the operating system is symbolic of a path in the wilderness. You need to follow the path to get to where you want to be. The PATH environment variable is like a map to tell the operating system where you want to be able to go. To view the directories in your PATH, use the echo $PATH command. This will display the locations of all commands you can run without telling UNIX where to look for them. The format of the listing is directory paths delimited or separated by the colon character (:). If a directory is not in your PATH variable, then you will not be able to find it or execute commands that reside in the directory unless you explicitly tell the operating system where it is. Such explicit directions are called absolute paths.

An absolute path refers to a location somewhere in a systems hierarchical structure. The reference always begins with the root directory (represented by /) and then builds a path to its destination file or directory. An absolute path is really the most accurate way to reference system locations when used with the cd (change directory) command, within a configuration file, or as part of a script. So, as an example, if you wanted to cd to /usr/local/bin from /var/tmp, you would simply use the following command syntax: cd /usr/local/bin.

A relative path starts in your current working directory. So use the pwd command to establish where to start your relative command from. As an example, if you wanted to change to the directory /usr/local/bin from /var/tmp, you could simply use the following relative command syntax: cd ../.. /usr/local/bin. The preceding command syntax is telling the operating system that you want to back up two directories and then go forward three directories to /usr/local/bin.

By this time you know what a directory is, but as a point of clarification there are a few terms used when referring to directories that need to be understood. The working directory is where you are where ever that may be. The pwd command will display or "print" you working directory to your screen.

The term *print* is used in the print working directory command because when UNIX was created, the printer was the system visual interface. You could not see what you were doing on a monitor like you can today. So use the pwd command if you get lost to find out exactly where you are in the system directory structure.

The term *parent directory* refers to the directory one level up from your working directory. So, if your' working directory is /usr/local/bin, then the parent directory would be /usr/local. A *child directory* is any directory that is located inside a parent directory.

A *filesystem* is a section of disk space that has been defined to the operating system. The disk space does not all need to be on the same physical disk. Nor does it need to be local to the machine the filesystem is defined on. The disk may be part of an external disk or disk array. It may also be located on another server. The only requirement is that the disk is accessible so that the operating system can access it. The filesystem definition includes information like the name of the filesystem, the absolute path of the mount point, the disk volume that the filesystem resides on, and whether or not the filesystem should automatically be mounted at boot time.

All filesystems have a mount point. A *mount point* is the directory in which the filesystem begins. So before you can mount a filesystem, you need to make the mount point directory. Do not put files in the directory before the filesystem is mounted. If you do, they will be covered up by the filesystem.

They will still be there, but you will not be able to access them until you unmount the filesystem.

The syntax to mount a directory is just the mount command followed by the filesystem name and then the mount point. So if I wanted to mount a cdrom on a mount point called /mnt, I would use the (mount cdrom /mnt) command. You would only need to mount a filesystem manually if it where new, or you had it defined to not mount automatically at boot time.

There is more than one type of filesystem. Some of the popular ones that you are likely to run into on UNIX are UNIX filesystems (ufs); Journaled filesystems (jfs); Network filesystems (nfs); and CDrom filesystems (cdrfs); (ext2), the default filesystem type for many Linux distributions; (ext3), which is essentially ext2 plus journaling; (devfs), a special filesystem for devices; and (proc), which is a special filesystem that does not actually exist on disk but is created virtually on the fly by the Kernel.

There are several commands that deal directly with the creating, manipulating, and viewing of filesystem information. The specific flavor of UNIX you are using may provide slightly different utilities, but they will perform the same tasks. To define a new filesystem, AIX uses the crfs command, while Solaris uses the mkfs command. AIX also offers the chfs command to change and the lsfs command to view the properties of a filesystem. They both offer the df command to view the status of mounted filesystems.

The df command is primarily used to keep track of what percentage of allocated disk space is still available. The df command by default displays the remaining disk in 512-byte blocks. Most people combine the df command with the –k option because that will display in 1024-byte blocks, which is equal to a megabyte. Solaris also offers the –h option to the df command, which displays in human readable form. That means that it lists the output with the appropriate notation of K for kilobytes, B for bytes, or G for gigabytes. That tends to be considerably easier than doing the math when the df command displays the available disk space in a seven-digit 512-byte block number.

The *inode* is a little guy that keeps track of information about your files. I have heard that the term inode is an acronym for I'm Not Operating DOS

Ever, but it is more likely that it refers to something to do with operating system indexes. The subject of inodes will no doubt get the attention of and impress the other geeks at a party, primarily because inode is a bit of a buzz word in UNIX crowds. The truth is, when cornered, most UNIX users would not be able to give you an adequate explanation about what an inode is or what it is used for. For that you would probably need to find a seasoned system administrator.

Every file or directory is assigned its own inode. The inode stores information like the size of a file; the UID of the file's owner; the GID of the files owner; a unique identification number called an *inode number*; the file's permission mode; some timestamps indicating when the inode was changed last, known as the *(ctime)*; when the content of the file was last modified, known as the *(mtime)*; and when the file was last accessed, known as the *(atime)*;and a counter that keeps track of how many links are pointing to the inode. Use the (ls –i) command to view the unique inode number for a file or the (ls –il) command to view a detailed listing of inode and file information. The information stored by inodes is defined by the POSIX standards for filesystem behavior. Adherence to these standards enables traditional UNIX utilities like fsck the ability to recover damaged filesystems.

Although a UNIX filesystem has a limited number of inodes, it is unlikely that this limitation will cause you problems. This is primarily because as in so many other settings with UNIX, the limit is set so high to begin with that it should never cause you a problem. If you are having filesystem or directory-related performance degradation, it is much more likely that your filesystem is too large or your filesystems are not laid out optimally on your disks. Poor filesystem setup can cause disk I/O contention, especially if the filesystem contains a database or some other I/O intensive application. That is not to say you can't build large filesystems. Large filesystems are quite common on enterprise-class servers, but large filesystems are usually used for large files, not a large number of small files. A few large files that occupy the same amount of disk space as many small files will use a fewer number of inodes.

A traditional UNIX filesystem does not have the ability to allocate additional inode space once the limit is reached. The filesystem attributes may vary depending on the specific flavor of UNIX and type of filesystem being used (jfs, ufs, zfs). If you suspect you are experiencing an inode shortage problem, use the (df –i) command to display the number of free inodes for your filesystem. If you do run out of inodes, the command or application being used when the inode limit is reached will generate an error message from the operating system that refers to being unable to make a file. This is because all files are links to unique inode numbers. Whenever a program refers to a file name, the operating system references a table to look up its corresponding inode number. If multiple files in a filesystem have the same inode number, then they are hard links to each other.

The following short exercises will get you familiar with the commands you will need to know to navigate and manipulate directories. So if you have a UNIX system available, take the time to walk through the exercise. I recommend that you perform the exercises in this book in your home directory. That will prevent any permissions problems or accidental damage to system files. The (cd) command executed with no argument will take you to your home directory. To verify where your home directory is supposed to be you can execute the (echo $HOME) command. This will display the value of your HOME variable.

Depending on how the home filesystem has been setup, your home directory may be a subdirectory of /home or /export/home. Some system administrators will create home directories for users on one server that exists for that purpose. The home directories are then mounted with nfs to whatever server you log in to in the environment. The advantage of this sort of setup is that no matter which server you log in to, all of your scripts and personal files are there for you as well as any custom environment variables you have created. So every server will have the same working environment for the users. This also saves disk space that would otherwise be used duplicating files for users on every server they have a user account on.

Exercises for Filesystems, Directories, and Paths

1. What character represents the root directory?

2. What is meant by absolute path?

3. What is meant by relative path?

4. What is the $PATH environment variable used for?

5. What does the acronym NFS stand for?

6. What does the acronym JFS stand for?

7. What is the df command used for?

8. What does an inode do?

9. What command can be used to display what your home directory is?

10. What command can be used to view the inode information for a filesystem?

5 USERS, GROUPS, AND PERMISSIONS

Users

If a user is defined locally, then there will be an entry for the user in the password file. The password file is located at /etc/passwd or /etc/shadow, depending on the flavor of UNIX operating system you are working with. If your system has a shadow file, you should make any manual user account edits to the shadow file rather than the passwd (password) file. The system will automatically insert your changes into the passwd file for you. The purpose of the shadow file is to give you a place to work on accounts while the system is running. Since you are not actually working on the main passwd file, you do not interfere with users who are trying to log in to the system.

When you have completed your work and you saved the changes to the shadow file, the system will sync the shadow file with the passwd file, making them the same. If your system does not have a shadow file, you are stuck with editing the main passwd file. If this is the case, I suggest you make a copy of the passwd file before you begin and then make your changes to the copy. When you are finished, you can manually move the copy into place and save a version of the old passwd file. A copy of the old passwd file can really save your bacon if your changes cause a problem.

A problem with the passwd file can cause the system to hang when the system is rebooted. If this happens, the easiest solution is usually to boot the system from a removable media, like DVD or tape. Once the system is up and running from the removable media, you can mount the root filesystem in an alternate location and modify or replace the passwd file with the copy you saved before you edited the file. Most systems have an alternate boot location built in for you. Look in your root directory. If you see something like /a that has no apparent purpose, that is what it is there for. If you do not have such a directory, it is easy enough to make a directory. Right? After you fix the problematic passwd file, just remove the removable media and reboot the system. With a good passwd file in place, the system should boot without any problems.

The passwd and shadow files store the following information about each locally defined system user in a colon-delimited format.

Password File Field Identifications	
Field	**Description**
User name	The account name you log in with.
Password	The passwords are stored in an encrypted format. They cannot be viewed or copied.
UID	User ID - The system uses numbers to identify users. Each UID is unique and is associated with a unique user name.
GID	Group ID – The system uses numbers to identify groups. The group text description is strictly for system users.
Comment	The comment field is usually used to hold the user's complete name and company or team. (John Smith – IFMC).
Home Directory	The absolute path of the user's home directory.
Login shell	The absolute path of the user's default shell.

If a user is defined in ldap (Lightweight Directory Access Protocol), then the same information is stored on a central ldap master server. This allows the information to be shared to all servers in the environment. However, it does not mean that a user will have access to all servers in the environment. If you have more than a handful of UNIX servers, you should really be using ldap to manage the system users. If you are not using ldap and your organization has 100 UNIX servers, you will spend a great deal of time physically logging in to each server every time someone forgets their password or needs their access permissions modified. If you are using ldap, you can make all changes from one central location and the changes will be propagated out to all ldap clients automatically.

The Home Directory

A *home directory* can be on a local device or it can be mounted from another server. Keeping home directories on a central server and nfs mounting them to all other servers in an environment can be handy. NFS-mounted home directories allows users to have access to all of their files where ever they are logged in. Additionally, it stops users from asking the system administrator why there files were deleted when the real problem is the user cannot remember which server they were logged into when they created a file.

The home directory is where a user will be placed when they log in to the system. The home directory is where you should keep all of your files that you do not share with other users. Your home directory shares disk space with all of the other system users, so if you are not responsible about the housekeeping of your home directory, you may hear about it from other users or the system administrator when the /home or /export/home filesystem fills up.

Passwords

Use the passwd command to change your password. Any user should be able to change their password. However, non-administrative users do not have the ability to change other users' passwords. Password requirements can be configured by the root user.

If your system account is being managed locally, and you need to change your password, just type passwd at the command prompt. The system will ask you to type your old password for user authentication. If you type the old password correctly, the system will prompt you for your new password. After you type the new password, the system will ask you to type it again. If you type it the same, your password will be updated. If you get it wrong, the system will give you an error and you will have to start over. The reason the system asks you for your old password is to stop other users from changing your password if you should leave your login session unattended. If you cannot remember your password, you will have to ask the system administrator to change it for you. The root user is the only user who can change your password without knowing what the old password was.

If your system account is being managed with ldap, you will need to tell the system where the password repository is located before you can change your password (passwd –r ldap). When you use the –r flag, the system will check the ldap configuration to see where the password repository is and will change it there. An ldap account only needs to have its password changed on one server. The ldap repository will cause the new password to be used on all servers in the ldap environment. Passwords do not need to be changed on the ldap master server, but they can be.

Groups

The UNIX operating system uses Groups to identify users that have the same level of access to directories and files. System Administrators may use groups to identify users that are working on the same project or who have the same job title. Groups are an effective level of security that adds granularity to the overall system security.

Group permissions are the 5th, 6th, and 7th characters displayed by the ls –l command output. The group permissions may be changed with the chmod command. The group ownership of a file may be changed with the chgrp command by the owner of the file. The groups command may be used to display all groups a user is a member of. The groups command will display both locally defined groups as well as those defined in ldap.

The Login Environment (Startup Files)

/etc/profile

/home/username/.profile (Over rides /etc/profile)

These files are read every time you log into the system. The login environment is determined by variable settings in a system configuration file called /etc/profile. You may over ride these settings as well as add additional variables by adding them to your .profile in your home directory. The system does not make the .profile for you, but it looks for it. If a user does not have a .profile, they will just get the environment that is setup in /etc/profile.

You can display your current environment with the env or set commands. If you want to display one particular variable, you can use the echo command followed by a space, a dollar sign, and the variable name (echo $PATH). You can set variables within a shell after you are logged in without having them in your .profile, but they will only be available for that session. The following is an example of common entries found in a user's .profile file.

export PS1="$LOGNAME@`uname -n`:\${PWD}> "

export PATH=$PATH:/usr/local:.

export TERM=vt100

set -o vi

export EDITOR=vi

stty erase

Common Environment Variables

Environment Variable Descriptions	
Name	**Description**
DISPLAY	The place you want X window displays to be broadcast to.
EDITOR	The editor you prefer to use.
HISTORY	The number of commands the operating system will remember for you.

HOME	Where you will be placed when you login or type cd with no argument.
PATH	The order in which the operating system will search for files or commands.
PS1	Your command prompt.
SHELL	Your preferred shell.
TERM	What type of terminal you are using.

File Ownership and Permissions

The following three examples demonstrate the output from the ls –al command for a directory, regular file, and a symbolic link. The output is displayed both in the actual format as shown on standard output as well as in a 2 x 11 table. The table is provided for the sake of readability. The table provides a numeric key that identifies and separates the fields. Immediately following the examples is a field identification table that corresponds with the numeric keys in the examples.

Directory

drw-rw-r-- 4 fred dba 1024 Jan 21 08:25 documentation

d	rw-	rw-	rw-	4	fred	dba	1024	Jan 21	08:25	documentation
1	2	3	4	5	6	7	8	9	10	11

Regular file

-rwxr--r-- 1 fred |dba 54219 Feb 9 09:37 file1.txt

-	rwx	r--	r--	1	fred	dba	54219	Feb 09	09:37	File1.txt
1	2	3	4	5	6	7	8	9	10	11

Symbolic link

lrwxr--r-- 0 fred dba 38579 May 7 12:42 sample.txt

1	rwx	r--	r--	0	fred	dba	38579	May 07	12:42	sample.txt
1	2	3	4	5	6	7	8	9	10	11

Field identification table

File Ownership Field Identification	
Field Number	**Description**
1	Type of file. (- = normal file, d=directory, l = symbolic link)
2	Access permissions (r = read, w = write, x = execute - =no permission)
3	Permissions for members of group
4	Permissions for world
5	Number of links to file or directory contents
6	Owner
7	Group ownership
8	Size
9	Date last modified
10	Time last modified

11	Name of file

Every file or directory in UNIX has access permissions. There are three levels of permissions. The three levels of file permissions are read, write, and execute. There is actually another level of no access, but that is pretty self-explanatory, and having that level of access won't get you anywhere. It is important to note that the permissions are not tied to each other. In other words, a user may have any combination of read, write, and execute. They may have just execute, or read and execute, or read and write, or no permissions at all.

Permissions are defined for three types of users:

- Owner (The owner of the file.)
- Group (The group the owner belongs to.)
- World (All other users.)

Thus, UNIX file permissions are nine bits of information (three types of permissions for three types of users). Each of the three user types may have one of two values for each bit of information. The two values are denied access or allowed access.

File Permissions Notation

Text representation like "-rwxr--r--"

Displayed in UNIX long directory listings. It consists of 10 characters. The first character shows the file type. The next nine characters are permissions, consisting of three groups: owner, group, and world. Each group consists of three symbols: **rwx**, if some permission is denied, then a dash "-" is used instead.

Example: -rwxr--r—

Symbol in the position 0 ("-") is the type of the file. It is either "d" if the item is a directory or "l" if it is a link or "-" if the item is a regular file.

Symbols in positions 1 to 3 ("rwx") are permissions for the owner of the file.

Symbols in positions 4 to 6 ("r--") are permissions for the group.

Symbols in positions 7 to 9 ("r--") are permissions for others.

Translation of Text Notation	
Text Notation	Description
r	Read access is allowed
w	Write access is allowed
x	Execute access is allowed
-	Replaces "r", "w", or "x" if according access type is denied

Examples of text notation:

Explanation of Text Notation of File Permissions	
Text Notation	Description
-rwxr-xr-x	File, owner has read, write, and execute permissions, group: only has read and execute permissions, others: only read and execute permissions.
dr-x------	Directory, owner has read and execute access; group and others have no access.

Numeric (octal) representation like "644"

If a numeric representation is used, like in the chmod command, then it is in the octal format (with the base of 8), and digits involved are 0 to 7. Octal format is used for the simplicity of understanding: every octal digit combines read, write and execute permissions together.

Example: "644"

Here the first digit ("6" in the example) stands for rights of the owner, the second digit ("4" in the example) stands for rights of the group, the third digit ("4" in the example) stands for rights of the world or other system users. The following table shows what numeric values mean.

Octal to Text Translation With Description		
Octal Digit	Text Equivalent	Description
0	---	All types of access are denied
1	--x	Execute access is allowed only
2	-w-	Write access is allowed only
3	-wx	Write and execute access are allowed
4	r--	Read access is allowed only
5	r-x	Read and execute access are allowed
6	rw-	Read and write access are allowed
7	rwx	Everything is allowed

The following table shows some examples of the octal and text equivalent for owner, group, and world permissions of some files. The ls –al command can be used to view the text form of the permissions, while the chmod command can be used to change the permissions of a file. Unless you are the root user, you will only be able to change the permissions of files you have write access to unless you are the member of a group which has write permissions on the file.

Comparison of Octal to Text Values for File Permissions	
Octal Value **Text Value**	**Description**
644 rw-r—r--	Owner: read and write permissions. Group: only read permissions. World: only read permissions.
660 rw-rw----	Owner: read and write permissions. Group: read and write permissions. World: all types of access are denied.
700 rwx------	Owner: read, write and execute permissions. Group: all types of access are denied World: all types of access are denied.
755 rwxr-xr-x	Owner: read, write and execute permissions. Group: read and execute permissions. World: read and execute permissions.

Scripts and Script Writing

At this point in the book, you have read all you need to know to write a script. Do not be intimidated by the term *script*. You can write UNIX shell scripts. To do this, you need to know three basic UNIX concepts. The first thing you need to know is some UNIX commands and what they do. The second thing you need to know is how to use an editor. The third thing you need to know is how to set the execution bit on a file. By definition, a *script* is an executable file. So to create a script, follow these simple instructions:

1. Use the vi editor to open a new file.
2. Change to edit mode in the vi editor.
3. Enter a UNIX command or two.
4. Save the file.
5. Use the chmod command to set the execution bit on the file.

You now have written a script. Just type the name of the file, and it should execute the UNIX commands in the file. If you get a response that says something to the effect of "Script_Name not found". Then where ever you created your script is outside of the bounds of your normal search $PATH variable. Whenever this happens, just enter a dot slash in front of the script name like this: ./Script_Name This tells the operating system to execute the file by that name in the local directory where you are sitting.

Exercises for Users, Groups, and Permissions

1. What is the UID for the root user account?

2. Figure out how much disk space your home directory is using.

3. What command can be used to change your password?

4. Use three methods to determine what group you belong to.

5. What is the GID for your group?

6. Create a file called gfile, and change the group permissions to read, write, and execute.

7. Change the group ownership of the gfile created in the previous step to staff.

8. Create a .profile in your home directory (if one does not already exist).

9. How can you setup a variable called MYNAME to your first name in your .profile.

10. How can you set up a custom command prompt in your .profile?

6 BASH, THE BOURNE AGAIN SHELL

The *bash shell* is the shell, or command language interpreter, that will appear in the GNU operating system distributions. The bash shell is a sh-compatible shell that incorporates useful features from the Korn shell (ksh) and C shell (csh). The bash shell is intended to conform to the IEEE POSIX P1003.2/ISO 9945.2 Shell and Tools standard. The bash shell offers functional improvements over sh for both programming and interactive use. In addition, most sh scripts can be run by bash without modification.

The bash shell is quite portable. It uses a configuration system that discovers characteristics of the compilation platform at build time, and may therefore be built on nearly every flavor of UNIX. The bash shell ports to UNIX-like systems, such as Linux, and to non-UNIX-like operating systems, such as IBM's OS/2 and Microsoft Windows operating systems.

There are other shells available to users, many of which are installed as part of the UNIX operating system by default. Since the bash shell is so user friendly and is increasing in popularity, I have endeavored to focus on the use of the bash shell in all examples in this book where applicable. In addition to many other features, the bash shell includes the following useful features. There are entire books and websites devoted to the bash shell and its features. I encourage readers to pursue the subject of shell features further as it will undoubtedly make your user experience easier and more enjoyable as you use the UNIX operating system.

Featured Bash Topics:

1. **Editing and Completion of Commands**
2. **History and Command Re-Entry**
3. **Job Control**
4. **Arithmetic Functions**
5. **Brace Expansion**
6. **Expanded I/O Capabilities**
7. **Control of Built-in Commands**
8. **The Directory Stack**
9. **Prompt Customization**
10. **Security**
11. **Comments**
12. **Custom Attributes and Colors**

Editing and Completion of Commands

The bash shell offers a command-line editing facility, which permits users to edit command lines using familiar emacs or vi-style editing commands (see vi chapter for list of vi-style editing commands). Editing allows corrections to be made without having to erase back to the point of error or retyping a long and complicated command line. The editing facilities include a feature that allows users to complete command and file names with a single key stroke.

The bash line-editing library is fully customizable. Users may define their own key bindings. *Key bindings* refer to the action the bash shell will take when a key is pressed. The bash shell also has a number of variables that can be used to fine-tune editing behavior. However, custom keyboard mapping is not required. The vi-style editing commands mentioned earlier are perfectly capable of handling most command line-editing situations. The custom key bindings are simply offered as a matter of preference and/or convenience.

To see what the current function bound to a key or key sequence is, use the read command. The following is an example in which I used the read command to display the binding to the F12 key on my keyboard. Keep in mind that key bindings may be different for different keyboards. To use the read command, just type read at the command prompt and then hit the return key. The cursor should drop down to the next line without displaying a new command prompt. The read command is interactive. It will wait for you to hit a key, at which point it will display the binding. It will continue to do this until you escape out of the command by hitting the Control C key sequence or whatever the escape sequence is on your preferred flavor of UNIX.

The escape sequence is usually the Control key followed by a C, D, Z, or X. Just try them until one of them works. You will not hurt anything if you use the wrong one; it will just display some gibberish on your screen until you hit the correct escape key. The last two characters of ^C are not part of the F12 key binding. It is from my escape key sequence. The actual key binding from the F12 function key is the ^[[24~ part of the read command output. The first two characters of ^[that are displayed by the read command need to be changed to \e when used by the bind command.

#read

^[[24~^C

To change the function of the F12 function key in the bash shell, you would use the bind command. The syntax of the bind command is bind single quote double quote \e double quote colon key binding function to execute single quote. So to use the F12 key to recall previously issued commands, you would enter the following at the command prompt.

bind '"\e[24~": history-search-backward'

Now to recall previously issued commands, you can just hit the F12 key until you see the command you want. This binding will only exist in the current shell. If you want this key binding to take effect automatically, you can either set it up in your .profile or in the system init file. The difference is the system init file will do the key binding for all users and the .profile will only set the binding for your account. It is a good idea to reserve system init settings for features that must be used by all users. Things like key bindings and command prompt customization are really a matter of preference and should be handled in a users .profile.

History and Command Re-Entry

The bash shell history feature remembers commands or entire command strings entered at the command prompt and allows them to be recalled and re-executed. The history list may be limited or unlimited size. To limit the command history, you need to set the HISTFILESIZE variable. The HISTFILESIZE variable will tell the bash shell how many commands to remember. The bash shell allows users to control which commands are saved on the history list. Another bash variable that can complement the HISTFILESIZE variable is the HISTCONTROL variable.

By setting the value of the HISTCONTROL variable to "ignoredups", the bash history size is optimized by keeping only one copy of each command in the command history. The bash shell allows users to search for previous commands and reuse portions of those commands when composing new command syntax. In addition to recalling and resubmitting commands, you may also recall previously issued commands and modify them before execution. The history list may be saved across shell sessions.

Job Control

On systems that support it, the bash shell provides an interface to the operating system's job control facilities. The operating system's *job control facility* controls which processes take precedence over other processes. For example, the operating system performs regular housekeeping processes that have a low priority. If a user were to initiate a task that requires system resources, the operating system may decide to suspend the housekeeping duties until such time as the task needing the system resources is complete.

If a user has multiple processes running, the user may decide which of their own processes should have a higher priority than the user's other processes. By allowing the user to interface with the job control facility, the bash shell allows the user to direct the processes they own to be suspended and restarted or moved between the foreground and background.

Arithmetic Functions

The bash shell allows users to perform integer arithmetic in any base from two to sixty-four. Arithmetic expansion allows an arithmetic expression to be evaluated and the result substituted into the command line. Shell variables can be used as operands, and the value of an expression may be assigned to a variable. An arithmetic expression may be used as a command. The exit status of the command is the value of the expression. The following table displays arithmetic operators, a text description of the operation they perform, an example of how they may be used, and an expanded description to further explain the meaning of the example shown. The operators in the table may be used at the bash command prompt or within a script to perform one-time or repetitive arithmetic functions.

Arithmetic Operation Translations			
Operator	Operation	Example	Description
+=	Addition	x+=y	x=(x+y)
-=	Subtraction	x-=y	x=(x-y)
*=	Multiplication	x*=y	x=(x*y)
/=	Division	x/=y	x=(x/y)
=	Simple assignment	x=y	x=y

The bash shell has operators that are not listed in the previous table, but the table does include the operators required to perform basic arithmetic functions. To perform more complex calculations, use the man page to learn more about how to use remainders, "and" and "or", "exclusive or", and other more advanced features.

Arithmetic Functions (Doing Math with UNIX)

Although arithmetic operations are mentioned as part of the functionality of the bash shell, the following table includes a more extensive list of arithmetic operators from the C programming language, which is common on UNIX operating systems. If you intend to write or read scripts that perform calculations or comparison operations, you will need to use and understand the following arithmetic operators. This section assumes you already understand how to perform arithmetic calculations. The purpose of this table is simply to provide the proper translation of arithmetic symbols into a format the UNIX Kernel will understand. Most of the operators are the same operators you would have learned in public school; however, some are not. I have not excluded the common operators in order to provide a complete list and avoid confusion. Additionally, as a reader of technical

material, I enjoy finding tidbits that I already knew. So here you go. The +
symbol is the operator symbol for addition. For those of you who already
knew that, good for you. You are a more savvy UNIX user than you thought.
For those of you who did not know the meaning of the + operator, you just
learned something, so you are getting your money's worth from this book.

Arithmetic Function Symbols and Their Meanings	
Operator	**Description**
!~	Logical negation
*	Multiplication
/	Division
%	Modulus (Remainder)
+	Addition
-	Subtraction
<	Less than
>	Greater than
<=	Less than or equal to
>=	Greater than or equal to
==	Equality
!=	Inequality
<<	Bitwise left shift
>>	Bitwise right shift
^	Bitwise exclusive OR

	Bitwise OR
&&	Logical AND
||	Logical OR

Brace Expansion

Brace expansion is an easy way to generate a list of strings that share a common prefix or suffix. To generate the list of strings with a common prefix or suffix, just use the echo or some other output direction command and feed it your prefix or suffix with a comma-delimited list of characters enclosed in braces. The following example creates the strings bat, cat, hat, and rat by using the comma delimited list of (b,c,h,r) and the suffix of "at".

#echo {b,c,h,r}at

The result is: bat cat hat rat

The same rules for brace expansion apply when creating strings with both a prefix and a suffix. To generate the list of strings with a common prefix and suffix, just use the echo or some other output direction command and feed it your prefix and suffix together with a comma-delimited list in the middle of your prefix and suffix of characters enclosed in braces. The following example creates the strings man, min, and mon by using the comma-delimited list of (a,i,o) between the prefix of "m" and the suffix of "n".

#echo m{a,i,o}n

The result is: man min mon

It should be noted that although the examples provided for brace expansion use a single-letter prefix and or suffix, single-letter prefix and or suffix functions is not a limitation of brace expansion. The same process can be used to create strings with a larger prefix or suffix.

Expanded I/O Capabilities

The bash shell provides several input and output features not available in sh, including the ability to:

- Specify a file or file descriptor for both input and output
- Read from or write to asynchronous processes using named pipes
- Read lines ending in backslash
- Display a prompt on the terminal before a read
- Format menus and interpret responses to them
- Echo lines exactly as input without escape processing

Control of Built-in Commands

The bash shell includes several built-in commands to give users more control over which commands are executed, or more accurately, the command and built-in built-ins change the order in which the bash shell searches for commands. The enable built-in allows other built-in commands to be selectively enabled or disabled. On operating systems that provide the dynamic loading feature, new built-ins may be loaded into the current shell from an object file.

The newly loaded built-ins will have access to all of the active shell facilities. Clear as mud, right? Okay, think of a built-in command as something that is part of the shell itself. The shell already knows about it so when you ask for it to be executed, the bash shell just executes it right away without thinking about it. When a command is not built in, the bash shell has to fork a new process to look for the command. When it finds it, it executes it. So think of using the built-ins as taking out the middleman.

The Directory Stack

The bash shell provides a "directory stack", to which directories are added that you have recently visited. As you change your current working directory, the [pushd] builtin adds the directory to your directory stack. The [dirs] builtin displays the current contents of your directory stack. The contents of your directory stack may also be viewed by echoing the value of the DIRSTACK shell variable to your screen. Another built-in that is related to the directory stack is the popd. The popd built-in is responsible for removing directories from the directory stack.

It is easy to toggle between two directories in the stack. To move backward one directory in the stack, you use the cd command with two dots like ".." as your target. To go back two directories in the stack, just separate the dots with a slash like "../.." To go forward in the stack, use the cd command with ./next_directory as you target where "next_directory" is actually the name of a directory. The single dot before the slash in ./next_directory refers to the current directory.

The directory stack feature is handy when a person needs to frequently navigate back and forth between directories and having multiple tty sessions open is more trouble than it is worth. If you are working on a directly attached dumb terminal or with a console session via a lights out management interface, then you will be limited to one tty connection by the nature of your connection, and the directory stack will be your only convenient method of navigation between frequently visited directories. Without the use of the bash directory stack feature, you will need to retype the absolute path of your destination directory every time you navigate away from your current directory.

Directory Stack Navigation Examples

#cd .. (Go back one directory.)

#cd ../.. (Go back two directories.)

#cd ../../.. (Go back three directories and so on.)

#cd ./nextdirectory (Go forward one directory.)

#cd ./next_dirtectory/another_directory (Go forward two directories and so on.)

Prompt Customization

The bash shell allows the primary prompt and secondary prompt to be customized. The variable that controls the behavior of the primary prompt is PS1. The variable that controls the behavior of the secondary prompt is PS2. The bash shell will display the primary prompt when the system is at rest waiting for a command. The bash shell will display the secondary prompt when the system is waiting for further input. I like to define the primary prompt to display the userid I am using and the current working directory I am sitting in. These two pieces of information can be displayed with the PS1 shell variable as follows:

#PS1='${LOGNAME}@${PWD}>' ; export PS1

Some other popular information to display in the command prompt is the system hostname, OS level, and system kernel. The PS1 variable can be set dynamically in your shell or can be set in your .profile to make it take effect as soon as you login. You are not required to make the secondary prompt different from the primary prompt, but it is a good practice because it lets you know the system is waiting for you to provide further input.

Be sure to make the difference between the primary and secondary prompts obvious enough for you to instantly recognize which prompt you are at. The secondary prompt should be something basic like ">". That way as soon as you see the little arrow at your prompt, you know you either made a typo at your last entry or the system needs more input to complete your last request.

Security

One of my favourite security features provided by bash is the rbash, or restricted bash shell. The *rbash feature* is designed to put a user (usually a guest user) into an environment where he or she is very limited as to what they can do from the command line. This is a good environment to give access to a training user, auditor, or vendor that does not need to have full access to the system. When a user logs into a system with an account that is using rbash as the default shell, his or her ability to navigate around the system and write files will be limited. You may set a user's default login shell to rbash by modifying the shell field in the user's record in the /etc/passwd or /etc/shadow file.

The following items document the specific restrictions placed on users who use the restricted shell as their shell environment. The restricted shell disallows a user from doing the following:

- Changing working directories: cd is inoperative. If a user with rbash tries to use it, he or she will get the error message bash: cd: restricted.
- Redirecting output to a file: the redirectors >, >|, <>, and >> are not allowed.
- Assigning a new value to the environment variables SHELL or PATH.
- Specifying any pathnames with slashes (/) in them. The shell will treat files outside of the current directory as "not found."
- Using the exec built-in.
- Specifying a filename containing a / as an argument to the built-in command.
- Importing function definitions from the shell environment at startup.
- Adding or deleting built-in commands with the -f and -d options to the enable built-in command.
- Specifying the -p option to the built-in command.
- Turning off restricted mode with set +r.

The rbash restrictions go into effect after the user's .bash_profile and environment files are run. Therefore, a cautious system administrator will change the owner of the users' .bash_profile and .bashrc to root, and make these files read-only before granting the guest user access to the rbash controlled account. The users' home directory should also be made read-only.

This means that the rbash shell user's entire environment is set up in /etc/profile and .bash_profile. Since the user can't access /etc/profile and can't overwrite .bash_profile, this lets the system administrator configure the environment as he or she sees fit without the danger of the restricted user escaping to another shell or changing the configuration of their own environment..

I have used two methods to contain the actions of certain types of users. The first method is to restrict the user to a directory and place a safe set of commands for them to use in the PATH environment variable for the restricted account to use. The second method for containing the actions of users with limited access or authority is to create a screen the user can log in to where they can select actions from a menu. Such selections may include generating a specific report that has been designed for the user, viewing backup statistics, or viewing system logs.

If the screen and menu are written correctly, all actions should end with the user being placed back into the menu screen where they started. The only way for the restricted user to escape from the menu screen should be to select the menu option that terminates their session and exits them from the system.

Comments

The bash shell command line ignores everything to the right of a hash mark or pound sign (#). The same rule applies inside system files as well. Configuration files are documented by sections of text or comments that are preceded by the # sign to inform the system to ignore that line and let the user know the line is a comment. The following four examples illustrate how pound signs are used in a file to create a space where comments or notes can be made about the file and ignored by the shell. Note that everything to the left of the first pound sign is ignored by the operating system. The four examples are meant to demonstrate that white space, special characters, additional pound signs, and test are disregarded when they are preceded by a pound sign.

This is an example of a comment line.

#---|This is an example of a comment line.|---#

###################################

115

#This is an example of a comment line.#

###################################

#This is an example of a comment line.

Custom Attributes and Colors

This section assumes the use of a display capable of displaying the color spectrum as would be used by a Super VGA monitor. If you are using a dumb terminal where all text and characters are displayed in a single color, you probably will not be able to change anything with the LSCOLORS variable. A single color dumb terminal is often referred to as a green screen because they are typically black screens with green characters, but I have seen them with orange and white characters also.

The bash shell variable LSCOLORS allows the user to customize the look of the shell environment by setting different file types to different colors and attributes. A special attribute may include something like flashing, bold, or underlined characters. If you do not modify the LSCOLORS variable, the following table displays the default settings. The following table displays the file type identifiers that can be used with the LSCOLORS variable to alter the look of a VGA screen by changing the color attribute for the various file types:

LSCOLORS Environment Variable File Types	
Attribute	**Description**
bd	Block (Buffered) file
cd	Character device
di	Directory
ex	Executable file
fi	File
ln	Symbolic link
mi	Target of orphaned link (visible only with ls –l)
no	Default global setting
or	Orphaned symbolic link
ow	Other writable (o+w) and not sticky
pi	Fifo file
so	Socket file
st	Sticky bit turned on (+t) to inherit properties
tw	Sticky and writable

I usually change the directory "di" setting to 00 for white rather than dark blue because I work with a black background and I find the dark blue letters difficult to read in front of a black background. You should fool around with the colors to figure out what is most comfortable for you to work with and remember. The different colors also makes it easy to tell at first glance what files are executable, zipped, or directories. The following table displays the numerical color codes to be used in conjunction with the LSCOLORS file type identifiers:

Value	Description	Value	Description
0	Default color	45	Purple background
1	Bold	46	Cyan background
4	Underlined text	47	Grey background
5	Flashing text	90	Dark grey
7	Reverse field	91	Light red
31	Red	92	Light green
32	Green	93	Yellow
33	Orange	94	Light blue
34	Blue	95	Light purple
35	Purple	96	Turquoise
36	Cyan	100	Dark grey background
37	Grey	101	Light red background
40	Black background	102	Light green background
41	Red background	103	Yellow background
42	Green background	104	Light blue background
43	Orange background	105	Light purple background
44	Blue background	106	Turquoise background

Exercises for Bash - The Bourne-Again Shell

1. How can you discover what shell you are using?

2. What file contains a list of shells that can be used on the system?

3. What file can you use to tell the system to automatically place you in your desired shell environment when you login?

4. How many nested sub-shells can you run?

5. How do you return to a previous shell environment from a sub-shell?

6. What symbol represents the logical and condition when doing arithmetic in the bash shell?

7. How would you use the echo command to display the words pen, hen, and ten with brace expansion?

8. What environment variable can be modified to change the colors of different file types?

9. Which bash feature allows a user to set the precedence of a job over or under other jobs on the system?

10. What command do you enter at the command line to enter the bash shell from another shell?

7 MANAGING PROCESSES

A *process* is created every time a command is executed. In fact, depending on the command, you may initiate more than a single process. When you execute a command, your cursor will drop to the next line and sit until the process completes, unless you run your process in the background. It almost gives the appearance that the system is thinking about what you just asked it to do. When the process completes, your command prompt will reappear.

The *ps* command is used to display information about processes. When executed without any options, the ps command will list information about processes you own. At the very least, you should see a process for your shell session and a process for your execution of the ps command. If you have additional shell sessions open with the same user account or have background jobs running, you should see information about those processes as well.

When the ps command is executed with the –f option, it will display more detailed information about your processes. The ps command with the -e option will display information about all running processes regardless of who owns them. You can of course, combine options to do something like display detailed information about all running processes by combining the ps command with the options -e and -f.

The execution of large batch-processing jobs has traditionally been done at night or on weekends. Depending on your hardware and operating system, this may or may not be necessary. Since we are focusing on UNIX here, it makes sense to point out some features of UNIX that allow you to control the timing of job processing.

The first method is *background processing*. Running a process in the background refers to the ability to execute a UNIX command or script and walk away from it or even log out of the system without ending the process. When you run a process in the background, it is submitted, and then the operating system gives you back your command line prompt so you can continue with whatever it was you were doing.

The background process will sit out there and wait for system resources to become available. Normal processes will be given a higher precedence than background processes. Therefore, if a background process is using system resources and a normal process is started, the background process will give up its resources until the normal process ends. Then the background process will resume its processing and so on until it completes. A background process is initiated by following a UNIX command with a space and an ampersand (&) symbol.

The second method of controlling the timing of processes has to do with *sequential processing*. To begin a process immediately after the end of a preceding process, place a (;) semicolon character between the two commands on the command line. (command1; command2)

The third method of controlling the timing of processes has to do with parallel processing. To run two processes simultaneously, place an ampersand (&) character after each command on the command line. This essentially puts all processes in the background at which point the Kernel will share resources between them. (command1 & command2 &). The following table is a quick reference for the ps command and the most useful command options used with it.

ps Command Options		
Command	**Option**	**Description**
ps		List process table entries.
	-e	Display information about all running processes.
	-f	Display more detailed information about processes.

	-u	Display process information about a particular userid. You must specify the userid following the –u and a delimiting space.
	-x	Display all active processes accept those connected to an active tty session.
	-A	Display all active processes.

The Top Command

The UNIX [*top*] command is a neat little tool for monitoring the "top" processes in your system. In other words, it will display the processes that are using the most resources in your system. The default of top is to display the top 10 processes. The top command itself uses resources, so system administrators usually try to discourage users from running it because it is interactive. That is to say, it will constantly update the output to you screen. So it is as if you are constantly running the same command over and over until you terminate the top command from sending output to your terminal or tty session with the Cntrl-c key sequence.

The following is a sample of top output. Obviously this snapshot was taken from an idle system. As you can see the top processes are the nagios monitoring service and the top processes itself. If other system users were logged in running commands or system intensive applications were running like a database, those processes would be listed before the two monitoring processes shown in this example.

```
top - 02:46:15 up 1:03,  1 user,  load average: 0.74, 0.74, 0.32
Tasks: 113 total,   2 running, 111 sleeping,   0 stopped,   0 zombie
Cpu(s):  1.14%us,  2.7%sy,  0.0%ni, 95.9%id,  0.0%wa,  0.0%hi,  0.0%si,
Mem:    899072k total,   450444k used,   448628k free,    72472k buffe
Swap:  2031608k total,        0k used,  2031608k free,   293684k cache

  PID USER      PR  NI  VIRT  RES  SHR S %CPU %MEM    TIME+  COMMAND
 4317 nagios    18   0  4160  756  644 S  2.7  0.1   0:00.02 check_nt
 4236 root      15   0  2428 1032  808 R  1.4  0.1   0:00.25 top
    1 root      18   0  2176  656  564 S  0.0  0.1   0:00.40 init
    2 root      RT  -5     0    0    0 S  0.0  0.0   0:00.00 migration/
    3 root      34  19     0    0    0 S  0.0  0.0   0:00.00 ksoftirqd/
    4 root      RT  -5     0    0    0 S  0.0  0.0   0:00.00 watchdog/0
    5 root      10  -5     0    0    0 S  0.0  0.0   0:00.02 events/0
```

Killing Your Processes

A user cannot kill other user's processes. The exception to this rule is the root user. The root user is used by system administrators to manage the system. The root user has rights to control all processes. By control, I mean the root user can kill or cancel a process, or change the priority of a process. By running a process in the background, the process is lowered in priority.

The system resources will be used by higher-level priority processes until they are complete at which time lower-level processes will regain access to the system's resources like cpu cycles and memory. You can kill your own processes with the kill command. Occasionally the command will be accepted, but the process will not end. This usually means that the process has child process still running. If you still want to kill the parent process, you can use the kill command with the –9 option. This means to kill the process no matter what.

The syntax to kill or cancel a process is kill # where # is the Process Identification or (pid) number from the process table. You may also use the pkill command to cancel your own processes. The pkill command is used in the same way as the kill command, except you may substitute the process name for the pid. In the following example, the ps –elf command is used to generate process detail. The pid is 1001, and the process name is inetd.

PID	PPID	PGID	WINPID	UID	TTY	STIME	COMMAND
1001	1000	1000	155	500	1	Oct 6	/usr/sbin/inetd

The pkill may be used in two ways to accomplish the task of canceling the inetd process. Any one of the following three examples is a valid way for canceling the inetd process in the previous output:

#kill 1001

#pkill 1001

#pkill inetd

Zombies

Zombies are processes that seemingly will not die on their own and you can not kill them. Technically when a process is in the zombie state, it isn't really a process anymore, rather it is just an entry in the process table. It takes almost no system resources.

Typically a zombie is a program process that has died but has not yet given its process table entry back to the system. Once this happens, the process ID number can be reassigned to a new process. Sometimes zombies will hang around until the system is rebooted. At system boot time, the process table will be wiped clean by the init process, and the zombie will go away, along with any other processes that were running the last time the system was running.

Zombie processes are for the most part harmless but can be annoying. The presence of zombie processes is usually not detrimental to the operating system, they are just a pain for system administrators or anybody else who is trying to view information in the process table. Normal system and application activity does not spawn zombies. A zombie is usually created by the abnormal termination of an application or by a user killing its parent process.

Daemons

A *daemon*, pronounced like daymon, not demon, is a process that starts at boot time and runs in the background waiting for requests. Because the daemons are initiated at boot time and are system related, the daemon processes are owned by the root user. A normal user should not be able to terminate a daemon process.

If a daemon process is killed, the daemon process can be easily restarted by the system administrator. However, most of the time daemons will restart on their own. The term used to describe a daemon or any other process restarting itself is called *re-spawning*. By convention the names of most daemons end with the letter "d". This naming convention makes daemon processes pretty easy to identify in a process table listing. Additionally, the names of the daemons are usually fairly intuitive of what they are for.

Examples of daemons are ntpd and syslogd. It is pretty easy to figure out what these two daemons are for. Right?

The ntpd daemon runs in the background and checks in frequently with the network time server. By using the network time protocol, the system clock is constantly in sync with all other servers on the network. Accurate system time is very important for logging and applications like databases that depend on accurate time to maintain the state of the database. Don't believe me? Try this little exercise on a **test system**.

Find a database that is actively logging transactions and shut it down with the normal shutdown process. (You may need a database administrator to help you with this part.) Then manually set the system time to a time between the time the database last started and the time you shut the database down. Usually, the database will detect the time discrepancy and refuse to start. If it does start, it will be in an unhappy state because it will have logged transactions that took place after the current time.

Exercises for Managing Processes

1. How can you list all of your processes?

2. How can you list all of your processes details?

3. How can you list all active processes?

4. What does the PPID column header stand for in the process table listing?

5. How can you end a process that you own?

6. How can you force a process to end even if it has dependencies?

7. What is the term used to describe processes that will not die?

8. How can you get rid of processes that will not die?

9. What user can manage any process?

10. What will happen if you end your own tty process?

8 MISCELLANEOUS UNIX UTILITIES

The following are some of the many utilities / commands that are part of most mainstream flavors of UNIX. Like any other UNIX command, these utilities exhibit different behaviors based on the options the utility is executed with. Therefore, the following descriptions and examples of how to use the utilities include basic options that a UNIX user or administrator should learn. The list of options is not all-inclusive because of the differences between flavors and versions of UNIX.

For a brief synopsis of available options with UNIX commands and utilities, try using the -h or --h (two dashes) options to display help. Many UNIX commands have the h option reserved for help. Usually the help consists of a list of available options with a brief description. Once you have tried these utilities out, you should look at the man page for the utilities on your operating system to see what additional options, features, and related commands are available.

Most of the following utilities and commands include a table of useful options that may be executed to enhance or modify the output. It should be noted that although the options are listed individually for clarity, they can be executed together. You should try the options individually and then in different combinations to see which output format you find useful and easiest to read.

The bc (Boolean Calculator) Command

Use the [bc] command to run the Boolean calculator utility to perform mathematical functions. The bc utility is handy for calculating large numbers because it can handle whatever numbers you can fit into your systems RAM and swap space. The bc utility can accomplish some very complicated calculations with the use of options, variables, and math library files if defined and requested on the command line. That being said, the purpose of this section is to make you aware of the bc utility and demonstrate some basic mathematical functions.

If you are interested in learning more about the bc command, I encourage you to look up the man page for bc. Before long you will be hammering out extensive formulas on the command line that look much like C programming language functions. This is because bc and C have similar syntax. You will find some useful options for the bc utility in the following table.

bc Command Options	
Option	**Description**
-h	Help
-i	Interactive mode.
-l	Define the math library.
-q	Quiet mode. (Skip the welcome message.)
-v	Display the version of bc you are using.
-w	Display warnings.

The most basic element in bc is the number. Numbers are displayed in decimal format and all computation is done in decimal. There are two attributes of numbers, the length and the scale. The *length* is the total number of digits in a number and the *scale* is the total number of digits after the decimal point. The following two examples demonstrate the length and scale attributes.

Example 1: 123456

Example 2: 1234.56

The first example shows a number with a length of six. The second example shows a number with a length of six and a scale of two. This means that there are six digits in the number with four of the digits to the left of the decimal and two digits to the right of the decimal. The first example also has a scale value, but the value is zero so it is not necessary to tell bc about it.

The following examples demonstrate some simple addition, multiplication, and division calculations with bc with and without using the scale attribute. Start by entering bc on the command line and then hit the return key. Then enter the numbers separated by the calculation symbol you want to perform and hit the enter key again.

The command prompt will stay in bc mode until you use the Control-d key sequence to escape back to the regular UNIX command prompt. If you want to use the scale attribute, you need to enter it before the calculation is performed, then hit enter and enter your numbers separated by the calculation symbol. The result to the calculation will be displayed in decimal format with the scale you asked for.

Use the bc utility to add two whole numbers.

#bc

2+2

Use the Cntrl-d key sequence to quit.

Use the bc utility to multiply two whole numbers.

#bc

2*2

Use the Cntrl-d key sequence to quit.

Use bc to divide 100 by 3 and display the result with 2 decimal places to the right of the decimal.

#bc

scale=2

100/3

Use the Cntrl-d key sequence to quit.

The cal (Calendar) Command

The [*cal*] or calendar command can be used to display a one month calendar for any month in the past, present day, or future. If executed with no argument cal will display the calendar for the current month based on the system clock. If executed with the argument of cal 7 1776, the cal command will display the calendar for July 1776. If executed with the argument of cal 12 3000, the cal command will display the calendar for December 3000. You can have some fun with the cal command. I like to use it to see what day of the week my birthday and holidays will be on the following year.

Use the calendar to show what day of the week the fourth of July was on in the year 1776.

#cal 7 1776

   July 1776

Su Mo Tu We Th Fr Sa

    1 2 3   4 5 6

 7 8 9 10 11 12 13

14 15 16 17 18 19 20

21 22 23 24 25 26 27

28 29 30 31

The date Command

To display the current time and date with the [*date*] command, just type the word date at the command prompt and hit the return key. The system will respond with what it thinks is the current time and date. The information displayed is the three-letter abbreviation for the day of the week, the three-letter abbreviation for the current month, the day of the month, the time in 24 hour format displayed with hours, minutes, and seconds separated by colons, the three-letter abbreviation for the time zone selected for the system, and the year displayed in four digits. The following shows an example of the date command being executed without any options:

#date

Tue Sep 28 19:35:26 CDT 2010

The date command may also be used to set the system time and date. To set the system time or date, type the date command at the command prompt, followed by the time and date information in the format of MMDDhhmmCCYY and hit the return key. The following table explains the format for setting the time and date.

date Command Syntax Description	
Code	**Description**
MM	Two-digit number for month.
DD	Two-digit day of the month.
hh	Two-digit hour of the day in 24 hour format.
mm	Two-digit minute of the hour in 0-59 format.
CC	Two-digit century.
YY	Two-digit year of the century.

To set the time to January 15, 2025 at 03:45:00 use the following syntax;

#date 011503452025

Wed Jan 15 03:45:00 CST 2025

The UNIX Graphical User Interface (GUI), X, and Window Managers

It is important to recognize that in UNIX operating systems, the GUI is separate from the operating system itself. This is unlike Microsoft Windows operating systems, which won't run without the GUI (or at the very least is extremely crippled if you do so). The GUI on UNIX is a separate layer that sits on top of the core operating system. The GUI can be completely uninstalled from UNIX, and you would still have a completely functional operating system.

I worked with UNIX for several years before my employer even had the software and hardware necessary to run the GUI and never had a situation that required a GUI. These days, whenever I am faced with using a system console that launches a GUI, the first thing I do is find the utilities menu and open the command window interface. Then I can use real UNIX commands to talk straight to the Kernel and get some real work done or have some real fun, whatever the case may be.

Version 11 of the X Window System is the underlying graphics layer on most modern UNIX systems. "X Windows," or "X11," or just "X" as it is commonly called, provides the glue between the underlying operating system, graphical applications, and graphics hardware. There are many software applications that are written for the X window system.

X by itself is not a GUI. Rather, X provides the facilities that a GUI requires - namely the ability to accept input from devices like a mouse and keyboard, and the ability to draw graphical objects to a display. So, despite its name, the X Window System cannot draw "windows," at least not by the modern definition of a window. This is the job of another piece of software called the *window manager*. There are many different window managers available for X. Some of these are proprietary and will only run on a particular type of UNIX. Some of these are open and will run on any system that has X installed.

For the most part, the window manager is what defines the look and feel of an X-based GUI. It provides features such as window frames and buttons, window titles, window resizing, icons, toolbars, desktop backgrounds/menus, and many other user interface elements. Some window managers also ship with their own set of desktop applications like file browsers, mail clients, and other common utilities.

Because the window manager is just a piece of software that sits on top of X, there may be several different GUIs to choose from on a given UNIX system. Linux systems, in particular, often have a number of different GUIs to choose from at the console login screen (or via some other mechanism once you've logged in).

There are many window managers available for UNIX systems. Because of the open-source nature of UNIX, most window managers either work on all UNIX systems out of the box or can be configured to do so with a little effort. The CDE, KDE, and Gnome window managers tend to be more widely used than others. Their popularity is largely because of their pleasant and intuitive feel and functionality. They are also widely available either on the Internet or come pre-bundled with popular flavors of UNIX.

The *Common Desktop Environment - CDE* is an open standard that has had some commercial success. Parts of CDE grew out of an older desktop environment called Motif. CDE ships, or has shipped, with Sun, HP, and IBM workstations. CDE is available from commercial sources for other operating systems such as Linux.

The *K Desktop Environment* otherwise known as *KDE* is an open source desktop environment for UNIX systems. KDE is included with some distributions of Linux as the default window manager. KDE is open source and can be used on any UNIX/X11 system. Due to its open source roots, KDE is primarily used on free UNIX operating systems such as Linux and FreeBSD.

The *Gnome* window manager is an open source desktop environment for UNIX systems that competing with KDE for the title of most popular window manager in the open systems community. Gnome is included with some distributions of Linux as the default window manager. Like KDE, Gnome is open source and can be used on any UNIX/X11 system. Due to its open source roots, Gnome has up to now been primarily used on free UNIX operating systems. Sun Microsystems has recently announced that Gnome will ship with Solaris as the default window manager.

The iostat (Input/Output Statistics) Command

As the name suggests, the [*iostat*] command is used to report input / output statistics as well as cpu, devices, and partition information. The simplest way to use the iostat command is to type iostat followed by a space, a number, another space, and another number and hit the enter key. The first number is the delay key and the second number is the number of lines of information to display.

So if you were to enter iostat 2 3 and hit the return key, the system would respond with three lines of statistics displayed two seconds apart as follows. It should be noted that the first line of the report is an average since the last system boot. Each line of the report after the first line is an average since the last report line interval.

#iostat 2 3

tty		dad0			dad1			ramdisk1			sd1			cpu			
tin	tout	kps	tps	serv	kps	tps	serv	kps	tps	serv	kps	tps	serv	us	sy	wt	id
0	10	158	14	25	608	53	35	0	0	0	0	0	7	46	37	0	18
0	119	24	1	4	68	1	21	0	0	0	0	0	0	65	35	0	0
0	40	145	25	4	40	3	7	0	0	0	0	0	0	66	34	0	0

The following is an example of the iostat command option to use to display cpu utilization followed by the system output.

#iostat –c

	cpu		
us	sy	wt	id
35	38	0	28

The headers in the default iostat command without any options are explained in the following table. The headers will change depending on what options you execute with the iostat command. For further explanation of headers and report column information, please reference the iostat man page on your operating system.

iostat Output Header Descriptions		
Device	Header	Description
tty	tin	Time receiving input from tty.
tty	tout	Time sending output to tty.
dad0	kps	Kilobytes read per second.
dad0	tps	Transfers per second issued to the device.
dad0	serv	Time waiting for service.
dad1	kps	Kilobytes read per second.
dad1	tps	Transfers per second issued to the device.
dad1	serv	Time waiting for service.
ramdisk1	kps	Kilobytes read per second.
ramdisk1	tps	Transfers per second issued to the device.
ramdisk1	serv	Time waiting for service.
sd1	kps	Kilobytes read per second.
sd1	tps	Transfers per second issued to the device.
sd1	serv	Time waiting for service.
cpu	us	Time spent running non-Kernel code.
cpu	sy	Time spent running Kernel code.
cpu	wt	Time spent waiting for IO.
cpu	id	Time spent idle.

The following is a table that includes common options executed with the iostat command to collect various bits of statistical information related to specific devices. These types of options are handy to make scripts with. For example, you could make a script called check_disks that collects all sorts of disk information and then use sed and awk (I know I did it too) to manipulate and format the output into a nice-looking report that runs on a weekly schedule.

Keep it to yourself and your boss will think you are some kind of genius when you are able to warn him or her in advance that a disk is about to go bad. Usually you will begin to see intermittent read and write errors before a disk needs to be replaced. With this information, you can have parts on hand or schedule the maintenance without experiencing any unexpected down time.

Most IT bosses love it when you can bring to their attention information that helps them look good by preventing system unavailability. It is much better to replace a disk on your terms than to deal with a system problem that is caused by a failed disk. When you replace a disk before it dies on its own, you are much less likely to lose any data.

iostat Command Options	
Option	**Description**
-c	Display CPU information.
-d	Display disk information.
-e	Display device error information.
-m	Display filesystem mount point information.
-n	Display device names in a descriptive human readable format.
-p	Display disk partition information.
-x	Display extended disk information.

-z	Do not display lines of information where all statistics report zero.

The sar (System Activity Reporter) Command

Use the [sar] system activity reporter to collect and display information from operating system cumulative activity counters. You do not have to set these counters up. They are constantly collecting information and refreshing themselves. However, you may save sar output to a file for later reference or multiple files for comparison and analysis of system trends. The following example demonstrates how to use sar with the –r option to retrieve and display unused memory statistics with 3 samples 4 seconds apart.

#sar –r 4 3

00:20:28 freemem freeswap

00:20:32 139528 2734464

00:20:36 139527 2734464

00:20:40 139527 2734464

Average   139527 2734464

The following table includes useful options for the sar utility. I have found that database administrators like to see sar reports. You will find that you and the people you support will be much happier if you can write scripts they can run on demand by themselves for database tuning or even just for their own curiosity.

If you find that you are writing a large number of report-generating scripts for users, you should consider writing a menu that users can launch and select scripts from. You will still have to set users up with permissions to access the menu and individual selections on the menu, but you will only have to do it once for each user. This is much better than manually running the save script for a user all the time. It will also put an end to users coming to you and saying, "Can you run that report for me" and expecting you to know which report they are talking about. Save yourself some time and empower your users to run reports themselves without bothering you.

sar Command Options	
Option	**Description**
-a	File access information.
-A	All data. (This is the equivalent of using all options together.)
-b	Buffer activity information.
-c	System call information.
-d	Block device activity information.
-f	Identifies a specific filename following the –f to be used as input.
-g	Paging information.
-k	Kernel memory allocation information.
-m	Message and semaphore activity.
-o	Directs sar to send output to a specific filename following the -o.
-r	Unused memory page information.
-u	CPU utilization information.
-v	Status of processes.

The split Utility

The [*split*] utility is used to split a file into pieces. Eventually, you will come across or create a file that is just too large to process, transmit, or store on portable media. For these occasions, the split utility is the perfect solution. The split utility can be used to split a large file up by size or line / record count. The syntax of the split utility is very simple and can be easily inserted into a script loop to split up one large file into several smaller files. The split utility will automatically name the output files with the name of the original file with an appended sequential suffix. The limitation of the split utility is 676 output files from one input file. The following table describes the options for the split utility.

split Options	
Option	**Description**
-b n	Split a file into pieces n bytes in size.
-b nk	Split a file into pieces n * 1024 bytes in size.
-b nm	Split a file into pieces n * 1048576 bytes in size.
-l	Split a file up by linecount..

The following is an example that splits a file called file1 into 100 line chunks.

#split –l 100 file1

The swap Utility

The [*swap*] utility is useful for managing and monitoring the system swap areas used by the operating system memory manager. Swap space is essentially the logical area the system associates to the physical memory in your system. You may also create swap space from disk space. You just need to create a disk partition and tell the operating system it will be used as swap. You then need to use the swap utility to add the disk partition as a new swap partition. Although swap space is essential for optimal performance of your system, be cautious not to create more swap space than you need with disk partitions.

Disk space is usually a premium commodity, and you do not want to waste it on swap space you don't really need. However, if you have the disk to spare, using a disk partition as swap space can get you by until you can purchase some memory for the system or migrate one of your memory-hogging applications to another server. Sometimes applications have what are referred to as *memory leaks*. Memory leaks that have been reported by enough customers are usually fixed by the next application patch set released, but you will have to deal with them while they are on your system.

Memory leaks are when an application basically is not managing the memory it is using optimally. The result is that the system memory eventually gets all used up. Rebooting the system will temporarily clean up the memory problem, but if you are running mission-critical applications, you may not be able to reboot your system. In this scenario, adding swap space may postpone the inevitable system reboot for a while.

swap Command Options	
Option	**Description**
-a	Add swap space.
-d	Delete the specified swap space.
-l	List the status of all defined system swap areas.
-s	Display a summary of system swap areas.

To display a summary of swap statistics, use the swap command with the -s option as demonstrated in the following example:

#swap -s

total: 476904k bytes allocated + 38800k reserved = 515704k used, 1367896k available

To display a long or detailed listing of swap statistics, use the swap command with the -l option, as demonstrated in the following example:

#swap –l

swapfile   dev   swaplo blocks   free

/dev/dsk/c0t0d0s1 136,9   16   1049312   1049312

The uname Command

The [*uname*] command displays the machine's unique hardware ID number. This is not the same as the frame serial number or part number for the operating system. The unique ID number is a combination of the hardware model, sub-model, and the ID of the server back plane. The unique ID for the entire system should be a 12-digit number.

It has been my experience that the first two digits are always 00. These digits are perhaps place-holders for systems with longer model numbers or for information that is not yet or has ceased to be included in the uname output. The following table explains which options to use to display specific system information with the uname command.

uname Command Options	
Option	**Description**
-a	All information.
-n	Node name.
-m	Machine ID number.
-p	Architecture of system processor (SPARC, RISC, AMD, Intel).
-v	Operating System version.
-X	Number of CPUs.

The uptime Command

The [*uptime*] command will tell you how long the operating system has been running or in other words, how long it has been since the last system reboot. The uptime output includes the current time and a count of days since the last system reboot unless the system has been rebooted within the previous 24 hours. If the system has been rebooted within the previous 24 hours, the time since the last reboot is displayed in hours, minutes, and seconds. The uptime command also displays the number of users that are currently logged in. The last bit of information the uptime command provides is the average number of jobs in the system run queue during the previous one, five, and 15-minute intervals.

The following uptime output indicates the system has been recently rebooted as indicated by the output in the format of hours, minutes, and seconds rather than in days. As you can see, since this system is only being used to host some lightweight web applications and to write this book, there is very little load reported by the uptime command.

#uptime

01:26:02 up 1:00, 1 user, load average: 0.10, 0.05, 0.15

The vmstat (Virtual Memory Statistics) Command

The [*vmstat*] command is used to display information about the current status of the system's active processes, memory, swap space, I/O (Input and Output), system, and CPUs. The simplest way to use the vmstat command is to type vmstat followed by a space, a number, another space, and another number and hit the enter key. The first number is the delay key and the second number is the number of lines of information to display.

So if you were to enter vmstat 2 3 and hit the return key, the system would respond with three lines of statistics displayed two seconds apart as follows. It should be noted that the first line of the report is an average since the last system boot. Each line of the report after the first line is an average since the last report line interval. So if you want to see 3 current average lines of output, you should request 4 for the number of samples and disregard the first line as it is not really current data.

#vmstat 2 3

```
procs -----------memory----------  ---swap-- -----io---- --system-- -----cpu------
 r  b  swpd  free   buff  cache  si so  bi  bo   in  cs us sy  id wa st
 0  0    0 446552 68624 296708  0   0  180  32   79  97 1 1   95 3 0
 0  0    0 446552 68624 296736  0   0   0    0   71  75 0 0  100 0 0
 1  0    0 446120 68628 296836  0   0  48   60   99 131 0 2   91 6 0
```

The second line of the two-line header of the vmstat command is somewhat cryptic. Therefore, please refer to the following table for a clear explanation of what each column of data represents as explained in the vmstat man page.

vmstat Output Header Descriptions	
Header	**Description**
r	Number of processes waiting for run time.
b	Number of processes in uninterruptible sleep.
swpd	Amount of virtual memory used.
free	Amount of idle memory.
buff	Amount of memory used in buffers.
cache	Amount of memory used in cache.
si	Amount of memory swapped in from disk.
so	Amount of memory swapped to disk.
bi	Number of blocks received from a block device.
bo	Number of blocks sent to a block device.
in	Number of interrupts per second.

cs	Number of context switches per second.
us	Time spent running non-Kernel code.
sy	Time spent running Kernel code.
id	Time spent idle.
wa	Time spent waiting for IO.
st	Time stolen from a virtual machine.

The wc (Word Count) Command

The [wc] command does what the name suggests. It counts how many words are in the file you feed it as input. If you just want to know the number of words in a file, then use the –w option. If you just want to know the number of lines in a file, then use the –l option. If you want to know both, then just use the wc command with no options and you will get both pieces of information.

wc Command Options	
Option	**Description**
-l	Display number of lines only.
-w	Display number of words only.

Use the word count command to display the number of lines in testfile.

#wc –l testfile

Use the word count command to display the number of words in testfile.

#wc –w testfile

Exercises for Miscellaneous UNIX Utilities

1. Using the bc utility, how do you divide 100 by 3 and display the result with two decimal places to the right of the decimal?

2. What is the key sequence used to escape from the bc utility back to the UNIX command prompt?

3. Use the calendar utility to show what day of the week the fourth of July was on in the year 1776.

4. What command can you use to display the current system date?

5. How can you change the system date to January 15, 2025 at 03:45:00?

6. What option is used with the sar command to display unused memory page information?

7. What command will tell you how long the system has been active since the last system reboot?

8. What information does uname –X display?

9. Using the word count command, how would you display only the number of lines in a file?

10. Which column in the vmstat output displays the number of processes waiting for runtime?

9 COMPARING, SORTING, AND COMPRESSING

This section is devoted to the various commands and the most useful options for comparing two files to each other, sorting files, and compressing files. The reason for comparing files should be pretty straightforward. There are other ways to tell if files are exactly the same. You can determine if two files are the same with the chksum value of a file. You can also look at the size, create date, line count, and word count of a file. Suffice it to say that there are many ways to determine if two files are the same. What we are going to cover here is how to tell what the difference is between two files.

The sort section is also pretty straightforward. The *sort command* is used for sorting files or the output of a command, but there is more to it than that. I will discuss different ways to sort files and output, including a built-in function designed for the sole purpose of sorting calendar files by month.

There are so many ways to compress files. I wanted to discuss each method briefly and help you identify which method creates and can be used to uncompress files with certain file extensions. File compression is useful for many reasons. Compressing files makes files easier to back up, easier to transport, easier to transmit, and saves disk space. Hopefully the compression section will provide enough of an introductory to file compression methods that you will be able to experiment with the different methods and select which method fits your needs or is at least the most comfortable for you to use on a regular basis. If you learn just one thing in this chapter, it should be that there are multiple ways to do things in UNIX

Comparing Files with diff

The *[diff] command* shows you what is different between two files. It is very handy once you learn how to interpret the output. The way you use diff is to enter the diff command at the command line, followed by a space, a file name, another space, and another file name.

The diff output will display an arrow pointing to the left "<", followed by data (text or numbers) that are located in the first file argument that are not located in the second file argument. There will be one of these left arrow entries for each difference found in the first file. The diff command will then display a dotted line to separate the output for the first file and the second file.

The diff command will then display an arrow pointing to the right ">", followed by data that is located in the second file argument that is not located in the first file argument. There will be one of these right arrow entries for each difference found in the second file that is not located in the first file. No output will be displayed if the files are identical. The following table includes some options for diff that you may want to try.

diff Command Options	
Option	**Description**
-b	Ignore trailing blanks.
-i	Ignore the case of letters.
-w	Ignore all blanks.

The following is an example of comparing a file called file1 with a file called file2. I will first show you the contents of each file to allow you to better understand and repeat the example.

The contents of file1 are:

One

Three

The contents of file2 are:

Two

Three

When the diff command is used to compare file1 and file2, the following is the result:

#diff file1 file2

< One

> Two

Since both files had the word "Three" in them, that word was not listed in the output.

Comparing Files with comm

The *[comm] command* is used to display data that is unique for each file in a comparison of two files. The default output of the comm command displays three columns of data. The first column of data will display data that is unique to the first file argument. The second column of data will display data that is unique to the second file argument. The third column of data will display data that is common between the two files being compared. The following table offers three options that may be used with the comm command to suppress columns of output. You may suppress more than one column at a time by combining the options on a single command.

comm Command Options	
Option	**Description**
-1	Do not display output for data unique to the first file.
-2	Do not display output for data unique to the second file.
-3	Do not display output that is common between the two files.

The following is an example of comparing a file called file1 with a file called file2. I will first show you the contents of each file to allow you to better understand and repeat the example.

The contents of file1 are:

One

Two

Three

The contents of file2 are:

Two

Three

When the comm command is used to compare file1 and file2, the following is the result:

#comm file1 file2

  1   2   3

One

       Two

Three

Note that since there is no data in file2 that is not included in file1, column two is empty in the output. Column one includes the word "One", which was unique to file1. Column three includes the words "Two" and "Three" because those words were common between file1 and file2. The output does not actually include numerical column headers. I have inserted the headers for readability in the example.

Comparing Files with cmp

The *[cmp] command* is useful for identifying the first location in which two files differ. The output of the cmp command includes the line number and character number of the difference between the two files being compared. The cmp command can be used in a script to test if files are identical. Beyond that, I find that the lack of descriptive output from this command to be a hindrance in my efforts.

Therefore, if I really want to find out what the difference between two files is, I opt to use the comm command instead of the cmp command. If the two files being compared do not begin with the same character, you will get a response similar to the following:

#cmp file1 file2

file1 file2 differ: char 1, line 1

This output is not very helpful is it? You can see if the first character is different in the two files just by looking at them. If you want detail, use the comm command. However, if you just want to know if the files are different or alike, the cmp command has an option that suppresses all output except the exit status of the command. You can use this in a script for a simple true-false logic. The following table includes two options for the cmp command that you may wish to try.

cmp Command Options	
Option	**Description**
-l	Display the decimal byte number and the differing octal bytes for each difference found.
-s	Return exit status only.

Sorting Files with sort

Sorting files is a common task. To accommodate this task in UNIX, we use the [*sort*] command. The sort command can be used to sort a file in a couple of different ways. When used with no options, the sort command will sort a file based on the first field in each line. To change this behavior, you use the "-k" option, which tells sort which field is the key field to sort the file on. You then follow the "-k" with a space and a number that represents the field you want to sort on.

If you would like to sort the file in reverse order, you will need to use the "-r" option. The "-r" option behaves like the default option of sorting on the first field in a line, except it sorts the file in reverse order. So if you want to sort a file in reverse order based on a field other than the first field, you will need to combine the "-r" and the "-k" options.

The sort command also has a reserved special option for sorting calendar files. The "-M" option will sort a file of months of the year based on their proper calendar order rather than the alphabetical order. In other words, when used with the "-M" option, sort is smart enough to put January before February and December last even though that is not their order alphabetically. The sort command will sort the contents of a file and display the output to your screen. If you want to save the result of your sort, you will need to use a redirection character ">" to send the output to a file. The following table includes the sort command with its options for quick reference.

sort Command Options	
Option	**Description**
-k	Key field identifier.
-r	Reverse sort order.
-M	Months.

The following examples demonstrate the correct syntax for the sort command with the discussed options:

Sort the file named months in the order they would appear on a calendar.

#sort –M months

Sort a file called testfile on the third field.

#sort –k 3 testfile

Sort a file called testfile in reverse order.

#sort –r testfile

Sort a file called testfile on the first field and capture the output in a file called sort.out.

#sort testfile > sort.out

Compressing Files

Compressing files and uncompressing files are things that users and administrators alike will need to do from time to time. Keeping things you are not using compressed helps to make optimal use of your storage on the UNIX filesystems and can keep people from pointing at you when a filesystem suddenly fills up. I am going to discuss what I believe are the most common compression tools in the UNIX world. The three methods are [compress], [gzip], and [tar].

The logic behind compression tools is pretty straightforward. They do not all perform the tasks in the same way, but essentially, the tool removes everything that you don't need to maintain the integrity of what you are compressing. Usually this means getting rid of all of the white space and other bits that do not actually hold data. Somehow the tools map where the white space goes and reinserts it when the files are uncompressed.

compress

The *[compress] command* is very straightforward. You just follow the command with the name of the file you want to compress. After you use the compress command to compress a file, you will notice that the file now has a ".Z" extension tacked on to it. This is handy because it reminds you later what type of file it is.

To uncompress the compressed file, you use the *[uncompress] command* rather than the compress command with an option. Don't ask me why this was done, but it works, so just remember it and move on. The following two examples demonstrate how to compress and uncompress with the two respective commands.

#compress filename

#uncompress filename

zcat

The *[zcat] utility* is used to display on standard output the uncompressed form of a file that has been compressed using the UNIX compress command. Using zcat is essentially the equivalent of using the uncompress command with the –c option. Using zcat to display the contents of a compressed file does not affect the compressed file.

zip and gzip

The *[zip] compression* tool, like the compress tool, has a companion command to unzip zipped files. You guessed it, it is called *[unzip]*. I like the zip command because when it makes the zipped file, it tells you how much space it saved. For example, if I ask it to zip a file called coins, it will respond with: adding coins (deflated 88%) or some other percentage, depending on the contents and size of the file.

The zip file needs you to tell it what to name the new zipped file it is creating because it does not simply zip up the original file. The zip command makes a zipped copy of the original file and adds the extension of ".zip" to the new file. So if your goal is to save space, you will need to delete the original file after you create the compressed zip file.

There is a newer version of zip out there developed by the GNU organization called *[gzip]*. Suffice it to say that it does pretty much the same thing zip does. It even has a companion command called [gunzip]. The gzip set of commands seems to be more popular these days because it is newer, which suggests it has improved upon the original zip binary. However, it is good to be familiar with both of them.

The most notable difference between zip and gzip functionality is when you gzip a file, you are gzipping the original file. So you do not end up with a compressed version of your original file in the same directory as your original file. You have the original file still, it is just smaller. Files that have been gzipped are easy to spot because they are given a ".gz" extension when they are created so you know exactly which tool to use to extract them.

If you care to examine the differences between zip and gzip beyond just how to compress and uncompress files, look them up with the man page on your system. The zip commands have plenty of options you can play around with. The following four examples demonstrate how to zip and unzip a file using the zip and gzip command sets.

#zip filename original_file

#unzip filename original_file

#gzip filename original_file

#gunzip filename original_file

gzip Command Options	
Option	Description
-l	List the compressed size, uncompressed size, compression ratio, and name of each compressed file.
-r	Recursively compress each subdirectory and file in the target path.
-t	Test the integrity of each compressed file in the target path.
-v	Verbose mode.

tar

The tar command is discussed in the backup section of this book. So to avoid a bit of redundancy, I will skip the detail of explaining the tar command and just demonstrate how to use it to compress and uncompress a file or directory. To compress something, use the "c" option, which stands for create. To uncompress a tar file, use the "x" option, which stands for extract. Notice I did not precede the options with a dash "-".

Unlike most UNIX commands, tar does not seem to care if you use a preceding dash or not. If you feel like putting them in there, tar will just ignore them, so it is up to you. I always include the "v", which stands for verbose because it streams the names of the files it is compressing as it does its job. You don't need to do that, but it makes me feel better if I can see what it is doing. The "f" option tells tar the next entry on the command line is the name of a file you want to compress.

It is important to note that tar actually makes a compressed copy of whatever you are compressing. The important thing about that is that the current directory or filesystem you are in needs to have enough overhead room to accommodate the original file, the new compressed file, and some work space for tar to do its job in. Similar to when you create a tar file, when you extract a tar file, it puts the original file back, but does not remove the compressed tar file, so you will need room for both files in the directory you are working in.

After tar is done making the compressed copy of your file or directory, use the "t" option, which asks tar to display the table of contents for the compressed file. The "t" option will display the name of the file, the permissions, and the date/time stamp for the file. If everything looks good, it is safe to remove the original file, and you have just saved some space or made your file easier to transport.

If you need to add a file to a tar archive after it has been created, use the "r" option. The "r" option is used to append new files to an existing tar archive. If you try to use the "c" option to add a new file to an existing tar archive, it will delete the existing archive, and the only thing in the archive will be the new file. Don't believe me? Try it out on a test archive with data you don't need to keep.

tar Command Options	
Option	**Description**
c	Create a tar archive file.
f	Identify the tar archive file.
r	Add or append additional files to an existing tar archive file.
t	Display the table of contents for an existing tar archive file.
v	Display verbose output for the current action.
x	Extract a tar archive file.

The following three examples demonstrate the c, t, and x options for tar. The v and the f options are also included, but I use them by default on all tar operations, because I always want to know what exactly happened and I want to control which tar archive file I am working with. Note that you need to tell tar what you want the compressed file to be called. I always stick an extension of .tar on the file names, but it is not a requirement. The operating system will always know what type of file a tar archive is, but adding the .tar extension will save you some frustration later when you are trying to work with the file. The following are some quick reminders for how to perform common tasks with tar.

Create a tar archive file: #tar cvf filename.tar filename

Display the table of contents of a tar archive file: #tar tvf filename.tar

Extract a tar archive file: #tar xvf filename.tar

Exercises for Comparing, Sorting, and Compressing Files

1. Compare a file called file1 with a file called file2.

2. Display the first difference between a file called file1 and a file called file2.

3. Sort a file named months in the order they would appear on a calendar rather than in alphabetical order.

4. Sort a file named file1 on the fifth field.

5. Sort a file named file1 in reverse order.

6. Use gzip to compress a file called file1.

7. Extract the compressed file1.gz file.

8. Use the tar command to compress a directory named /dir1.

9. Use the tar command to list the contents of the compressed dir1.tar file without extracting it.

10. Use the tar command to extract the compressed dir1.tar file.

10 BACKUPS

One of the most important duties I perform as a UNIX system administrator is to manage and perform backups and restores of system and user files. A system without good backups is a disaster waiting to happen. I say good backups because I have both heard and experienced what can happen when you think you have a backup of something only to find out your backup media or your backup logic is insufficient when you need it.

During my career as a UNIX systems administrator, I have had the opportunity to make backups with all kinds of devices from floppy disks to robot-controlled tape silos. Although I have used several different backup software packages made by various vendors, I prefer the tar command. Some of the reasons I like tar are because it is free, it comes with or is portable to all flavors of UNIX, and it is very functional and easy to use. Additionally, I have discovered that some fancier backup software packages run tar processes in the background anyway.

Take a look at your processes the next time a backup or restore job is running with some other backup software. You may be surprised to see a tar process out there doing the work. This is because vendors have developed GUI or web interfaces that are intuitive for users to operate to perform backups that use tar as a back end. After all, why should they bother developing something that already exists when they can just give it a new look and sell it?

The tar command was designed to make tape archive files. But it has since been widely used as a method to save collections of files and directories in the form of a single file as well as to compress files and directories. The tar command creates a file, it makes an index of the files to be archived, and it makes a copy of the data to be archived in its file. After the tar file is created, it can be zipped up to save space. This makes it easier to move and restore large groups of files.

To create a tar file, use the following syntax: (tar –cvf tarfile file). In the previous example, the word tarfile represents the output file or the name of the archive you are creating. I usually name them something that will help me remember what is in them. I also use the tar extension on the filename. This is not required, but it is a matter of convention. It tells people what type of file it is and lets them know what command to use to expand or restore it. The word file in the previous example represents the name of whatever you are backing up. It can be the name of a file, directory, or even a filesystem.

To restore a tar file, use the following syntax: (tar-xvf tarfile location). Restoring a tar file will recreate the files and directories contained in the tar file in hierarchical order. It will restore them to the current working directory unless you give it an absolute path of where to start restoring the files. The restore process with a tar archive does not remove the tar archive file. So what you will end up with is the newly restored files sitting in the directory with the tar archive if you put them in the same place. If you do not have room for both, you may need to put the tar file in an alternate location while performing the restore.

To display the index or table of contents for a tar file, use the following syntax: (tar –tvf tarfile). To redirect the index output from a tarfile into a file that can be later printed or viewed with other UNIX commands, use the following syntax: (tar –tvf tarfile > /tmp/index). To redirect the index output from a tar archive that is on a backup tape into a file that can be later printed or viewed with other UNIX commands, use the following syntax: (tar –tvf /dev/rmt0 > /tmp/index). This is a good way to verify that you backed up what you thought you did. It can also be used to check the contents of a backup tape. If you redirect your index output into a file and then name the file with a date, you will have a record of what was backed up that day. You should stick these index files in a directory called Backup_Logs or something like that so they won't get deleted and you know where to find them.

cpio

The *cpio utility* is also used to perform backups. The name cpio describes the commands function. It is used to copy file archives in and out of devices, another file, or a pipe leading to another command. The input and output can be read from and written to tape devices or other mountable media.

The cpio utility has many options that allow it to be quite a versatile tool, but personally I have never really acquired a taste for it. But that does not mean the utility is completely without merit. I have in the past worked with another system administrator who seemed to be quite comfortable with regular use of cpio to perform backup and data transfer tasks. I think he just liked to use it because it was the first backup method he was taught and he was comfortable with it. Like the tar utility, the cpio utility is free and comes with or is portable to all flavors of UNIX, so the choice is yours.

The cpio utility has three operating modes. The *copy-in* and *copy-out modes* copy files into an archive. It reads a list of filenames from standard input and writes the archive to standard output. An easy way to generate a list of filenames for input to cpio is with the find command. Just search for what you want to back up with the find command, and it will generate a list of absolute path filenames to feed to the cpio utility.

Another cpio mode is the *copy-pass mode*. It copies files from one directory tree to another, combining the copy-out and copy-in steps. The destination directory is given as an argument. I recommend using the find command output as input to cpio as the copy-pass mode is more difficult to use than it needs to be, especially if you have already mastered how to pass output between commands with a pipe.

The cpio utility creates binary format archives by default. For the sake of compatibility, the creators of cpio had the foresight to have it evaluate and automatically recognize which kind of archive it is reading.

The cpio utility creates archives in a slightly different manner than tar. While tar will archive everything from its starting point on down, including all subdirectories and their contents, cpio will only archive what it is exclusively instructed by the input list. To create an archive with the cpio command, use the –o (copy out) option. This will cause it to read a list of files from stdin, create the archive, and write the archive to stdout. An easy way to generate the input list is with the find command. To create an archive of a directory, including all of its contents and possible sub-directories, compress it with gzip and write the results to a file. The following is a syntax example of how to do this:

#find dir1 –print | cpio –o | gzip > dir1.cpio.gz

Just to clarify the preceding example, we started with a directory called dir1 that had some files in it. We wanted to create a compressed archive file of the directory dir1. We used the find command to send a complete listing of dir1 to cpio as input. We then piped the cpio archive to gzip to compress it. What we ended up with was a compressed cpio archive in gzip format called cpio.dir1.gz.

To perform an incremental backup with cpio of files that have changed from the previous day, use the following syntax: (find dir1 -ctime -1 -print | cpio -o |gzip >dir1.cpio.gz).

Using the find command to create the input list of files opens the door to your ability to be very selective in the manner in which you archive your files. A quick review of the find command should hopefully ignite some spark for a few ideas of how to generate a list of files based on age, location, owner or whatever else is relevant information at the time.

Once you have developed a few of your favorite ways to create file lists, it is a simple step from there to put those commands into a script and execute them whenever you want. You can even use the systems scheduler to kick off your backup jobs on a regularly scheduled basis. To extract files from an archive, use the -i (copy in) command line option. That will tell cpio to read an archive from stdin and to extract the files from it. So, assuming the archive is compressed, do this: (gzcat dir1.cpio.gz |cpio –i).

Although cpio archives are usually smaller than tar archives, the following example shows pretty clearly why I prefer to use the tar method over the cpio method when given the choice. As you can see, the following example performs the very basic task of backing up the contents of the current directory. The cpio command requires the help of another command and significantly more keystrokes to perform the same function.

find . -print | cpio -o >../archive.cpio

tar cf ../archive.tar

cpio Command Options	
Option	**Description**
-A	Append to an existing archive. Only works in copy-out mode. The archive must be a disk file specified with the -O or -F (--file) option.
-B	Blocking – Force a particular block size on a tape device.
-i	In – Run in copy-in mode.
-l	List – Print a table of contents of the input.
-o	Out – Run in copy-out mode.
-p	Pass – Run in copy-pass mode.
-R	Ownership – In copy-out and copy-pass modes, set the ownership of all files created to the specified user and or group.
-r	Rename – Rename files.
-u	Unconditional – Replace all files, without asking whether to replace existing newer files with older files.
-V	Dot – Print a dot "." For each file processed. This is used for a progress meter.
-v	Verbose mode – List the files as they are processed.

Moving Data Between Devices

Occasionally you may need to make tape-to-tape copies. This is a good idea both for redundancy as well as reclamation. *Tape reclamation* is done when you have several tapes that each have either small amounts of data on them or small amounts of relevant data. The idea is that you can transfer the small bits of data from several tapes onto one or at least fewer tapes, thereby reclaiming the wasted tape space. Hence the name, reclamation. An excellent utility for performing this tape-to-tape transfer is the dd command.

The *dd utility* is used to copy a specified input file to a specified output file. The files can be located on any type of accessible raw device. This makes it suitable to work with raw disks and tape drives. The input file is specified with the if= parameter, while the output file is specified by the of= parameter. If no input or output files are declared when the dd command is executed, standard input and output are used by default.

You may control the block size with the optional −b flag followed by a space and a number. Block sizes are specified in bytes. If you follow the block size number with a k, the output file will be made in 1024-byte blocks. If you follow the block size number with a b, the output file will be made in 512-byte blocks. The following example demonstrates the required syntax to copy a file called datafile from tape drive rmt0 to tape drive rmt1. The example assumes the naming convention used for raw tape devices is /dev/rmt#.

#dd if=/dev/rmt0/datafile of=/dev/rmt1/datafile

Since the dd command performs its function at a lower level than the standard UNIX cp command, it is better suited for copying entire disk partitions or entire disks. This makes it an acceptable option for system functions like backing up the boot sector on a disk. The cp command is well suited for this job because it does not copy disk space track for track. It merely copies the visible files ignoring white space, hidden files, and deleted files that are still present on a disk.

The dd command is sometimes jokingly referred to as the "Destroy Data" command. This is, of course, an incorrect but humorous description of the command's function. The command does have options that allow data translation from EBCDIC to ASCII and vice versa as well as case translation, but such functions are beyond the scope of this discussion. However, if a person were to make a syntax mistake like reversing the order of the input or output parameters, the result would be undesirable.

Another utility used for moving data between tape devices is the *tcopy command*. The only requirement for using tcopy is that the mounted source tape has two tape marks at the end. The two marks signify the end of file marker, which tells tcopy to stop. The tcopy syntax is very simple. It is as follows: tcopy source destination.

The source is the only required parameter. If you do not include a destination parameter, tcopy will scan the source tape and display statistics about the image to standard out. The statistics will include information about records found on the tape image, like record sizes. If you do specify the destination parameter, tcopy will make a copy of the mounted source tape to the mounted destination tape. The tcopy will display the tape statistics to standard out during the copy process by default.

Controlling Tape Devices

If you are not using a backup software package that controls your tape device for you, you may need to use the mt utility to manually control magnetic tape devices. The *mt utility* lets you give instructions directly to a tape drive. The command syntax for mt is (mt –f tapename command count). The –f flag tells the mt utility that the next word on the command line is the name of a tape drive.

You do not have to include this part if you only have one tape drive. If you do not use the –f option, the mt utility will use whatever is defined by the TAPE environment variable. If the TAPE environment variable is not defined, mt will assume your tape device is located at /dev/rmt/0n. The count parameter tells mt how many times to perform the specified command and is optional. If you do not specify the count parameter, the default is to perform the specified command once. The following table explains the commands that may be used with the mt utility.

mt Utility Commands	
Command	**Description**
eof	Write count EOF marks at the current position on the tape.
weof	Write count EOF marks at the current position on the tape.
fsf	Forward space over count EOF marks. The tape is positioned on the first block of the file.
fsr	Forward space count records.
bsf	Backspace over count EOF marks. The tape is positioned at the beginning of the previous EOF mark.
bsr	Backspace count records.
nbsf	Backspace count files. The tape is positioned on the first block of the file.
asf	Absolute space to count file number. This is the same as rewinding a tape and then moving forward with the fsf command.
com	Space to the end of recorded media on the tape. This is useful for appending files onto previously written tapes.
rewind	Rewind the tape.
offline	Rewind the tape and take the tape device offline.
rewoffl	Rewind the tape and take the tape device offline.
status	Display status information about a tape device.
retension	Rewind a tape, then advance it to the end of the reel and

	then rewind it again. This is done to relieve tape tension.
reserve	Allow the tape drive to remain reserved after closing the device.
release	Re-establish the default behavior of releasing at close.
erase	Erase the entire tape. Erasing a tape may take a long time depending on the device and/or tape. Refer to the device specific manual for time details.

I usually do not concern myself with the specific definitions of exit statuses because it is a general rule that an exit status of 0 indicates success, while anything greater than 0 is a failure. However, in the case of the mt utility, I make an exception because there are only two other possible exit statuses and knowing the difference between the two may assist in debugging a problem.

The exit status of 1 indicates that the issued command was unrecognized or mt was unable to open the specified tape drive for some reason. The reasons for getting an exit status of 1 are usually because you mistyped the command, the tape drive is powered off, or there is a communication problem with the tape device. A communication problem can take a few forms. It could mean that the device is not defined correctly, there could be an I/O cable problem, or the device may not be terminated correctly. The exit status of 2 simply means that the operation failed. This one is not very helpful, but at least you know you didn't type the command wrong. In this case, it is more likely that there may be a problem with the tape media.

Tapes do not last forever and they have their faults, but most of the time they work and they can really save you when those important files go missing or get corrupted. Some of the common problems with overused tapes are that they can break when they finish rewinding, and sometimes the see-saw effect of positioning the tape to find a record can stretch the tape over time. When a tape gets stretched, the blocking gets distorted and it becomes unreadable. New tapes tend to let some of the magnetic matter flake off the first couple of times they are used. This does not damage the tape, but the particles of magnetic matter get on the heads of the tape drive, which requires the drive to be cleaned more frequently. Remember to periodically clean your tape drive. It can save you from backup and restore headaches.

Earlier in this chapter, I briefly mentioned the system scheduler. In UNIX the scheduler is called *cron*. This stands for chronological scheduler. All system may use cron to schedule jobs as long as the crond daemon is running and the system administrator has not specifically denied you access to the scheduler by creating an entry for your account in the /etc/cron.deny file.

A user accesses the scheduler with the crontab command. There are two flags to be used with crontab. The –e flag allows you to edit your schedule, while –l flag simply displays a listing of your schedule. Never execute the crontab command without one of these flags. If you do this accidentally, don't panic. Use the Control – c key sequence to escape back to the command line.

Do not use the Control – d key sequence. If you do, you will find out the hard way that this re-initializes your schedule. In other words, it wipes out any entries your previously had stored in your schedule. The first time you use the crontab command, the system will create you your own scheduler file in the /var/spool/cron/crontabs directory. The files name will match your user name.

A crontab file consists of lines of six fields each. The fields of the crontab file are separated by spaces or tabs. The first five fields contain numbers that specify the following: The first field represents minutes and can contain a numerical value of 0 – 59. The second field represents hours and can contain a numerical value of 0 – 23. The third field represents the day of the month and can contain a numerical value of 1 – 31. The fourth field represents the month of the year and can contain a numerical value of 1 – 12. The sixth field represents the day of the week and can contain the value of 0 – 6. Just for the sake of clarity, I have defined the numerical day values for you. The numerical day values are 0 = Sunday, 1 = Monday, 2 = Tuesday, 3 = Wednesday, 4 = Thursday, 5 = Friday, and 6 = Saturday. The sixth field is where you enter the name of the executable file, script, or command line argument that you want to be executed at the day and time indicated by the first five fields of the crontab entry. For the sake of clarity, I have explained the fields of the crontab entries in the following table:

crontab Entry Requirements		
Field Number	**Field Name**	**Acceptable Values**
1	Minute	0-59
2	Hour	0-23
3	Day of the month	1-31
4	Month of the year	1-12
5	Day of the week	0-6 0=Sunday, 1=Monday, 2=Tuesday, 3=Wednesday, 4=Thursday, 5=Friday, 6=Saturday
6	Command	Executable file or command syntax. It is best to use the absolute path of executables in the crontab since you cannot depend on your shell environment variables being active when you are not logged in.

An asterisk (*) may be substituted for a number in any of the first five fields of a crontab entry. The asterisk represents a wildcard that represents all legal values for that field. So for field five which is the day of the week field, * and 0-6 and 0,1,2,3,4,5,6 all have the same meaning and are all legal values. The hyphen in the 0-6 example represents an inclusive range. In the previous example, the numbers have been separated by commas. You do not need to list a complete range of numbers to use the comma separator. You could have used 0,3,5 if you just wanted to execute a command on Sunday, Wednesday, and Friday.

A pound sign (#) identifies a comment in the crontab file. If the pound sign is in the first position on a line, then the whole line is ignored. If the pound sign is to the right of the command string to be executed, then everything to the right of the pound sign is ignored.

You may have noticed that both the third and fifth fields of the crontab entry represents days. If both of these fields include numerical values, the command string will be executed on both specified days. So if the third field has a 3 and the fifth field has a 2, then the command string will be executed on the third day of the month no matter what day of the week that is as well as every Tuesday of the month. If the third day of the month is a Tuesday, nothing special happens; the command string is executed only once that day. The following are a few examples of legal crontab entries:

10 3 * 5 * /usr/sbin/test_script1 # This script will be executed at 3:10 am every day of May.

30 20 * * 1 /usr/local/bin/test_scrip2 # This script will be executed at 8:30 pm on every Monday.

#10 22 * * * /usr/local/test_script3 # This script will not be executed because the pound sign in the first position identifies the line as a comment.

Similar to cron is the [at] command. Unlike cron, which is used to run jobs on a regularly scheduled basis, the at command runs a job once and then forgets about it. I recommend that new UNIX users use cron rather than at because the scheduled jobs are much easier to keep track of. If you still think you want to, take a crack at using the at command.

The syntax is pretty straightforward. You just tell the system at the command line that you want to execute something "at" a certain time. Like this: (at 0815am Jan 24 uptime >> howlong.txt). In the previous example, the uptime command will be executed and the output will be appended to a file called howlong.txt at the designated time and date. The at command also accepts common definitions of times in text format like now, noon, and midnight.

The privileges of the at command are usually more secure than the crontab because of the possibility of its malicious use. Don't be surprised if you get a message from the system like "at: you are not authorized to use at.

Sorry." when you try to use the at command. The privileges for the at command are controlled by the system administrator. To modify the privileges for a user associated with the at command, you must modify one of the following files depending on how the security has been setup for the at command.

/usr/lib/cron/at.allow and /usr/lib/cron/at.deny

or

/etc/at.allow and /etc/at.deny

If the at.allow file exists, then only users listed in the file are allowed to use the at command to submit commands for execution at a later time. The format of the at.allow file is one user per line. No white space is allowed inside the file. The root user is allowed to use the at command at all times, even if it is not listed in the at.allow file.

If the at.allow file does not exist, the system will check the at.deny file for a list of users that are not allowed to submit commands for execution at a later time. The format of the at.deny files is the same as the at.allow file. If the at.allow file does not exist and the at.deny file is empty, then all users are allowed to use the at utility.

The reason the privileges for the at command are so tightly managed is because once an at command has been submitted for later execution, it is not as easy to detect as a scheduled cron job that is plainly visible in the crontab file. Although the creators of the at command had good intentions when they created it, the opportunity for malicious uses of the at command is too great. For the sake of security and system stability, I recommend that the use of the at command be locked down. Failure to do so is an open invitation for a user to set a ticking time bomb in your system.

Exercises for Backups

1. What does the word "tar" stand for in relation to the tar command?

2. What is the –t option used for with the tar command?

3. What is the –V option used for with the cpio backup utility?

4. What is the –l option used for with the cpio backup utility?

5. What command can be used to move data easily at the block level between devices?

6. What is the name of the utility used to manage tape devices?

7. What does the rewoffl option do when managing tape devices?

8. What character is used to identify Tuesday in a crontab entry?

9. What is the fifth field in a crontab entry used for?

10. How can you view the contents of your own crontab without opening the table in edit mode?

SOLUTIONS FOR CHAPTER EXERCISES

1 – Solutions for UNIX Basics Exercises

1. ls *a*
2. command >> existing_filename
3. The Open Group
4. The "?" wildcard is used to match any single character.
5. Lower power consumption, lower heat signature, smaller physical footprint, and less expensive than a server or a workstation.
6. man man
7. alias (Executed with no argument).
8. env or set
   a.env | grep TERM or echo $TERM or set | grep TERM
9. A protocol is a set of rules that the operating system must use.
10. A protocol is a set of rules that the operating system must use.

2 – Solutions for Manipulating Files Exercises

1. cp file1 file2
2. mv file2 file3
3. rm file3
4. rm –r /tmp/
5. ls –a /var/tmp
6. man grep > grep.out
7. ls | grep –v 1
8. cp –p file1 file4
9. head –n 3 file1
10. grep a file1

3 – Solutions for Editors Exercises

1. Command mode and insert mode
2. dd
3. x
4. :q!
5. S
6. D
7. g following the last "/" slash.
8. $EDITOR
9. set –o vi
10. Esc k

4 – Solutions for Filesystems, Directories, and Paths Exercises

1. /
2. The absolute path represents the complete path of a file from the root directory.
3. The relative path represents the direct route to a file from the current location.
4. The $PATH variable holds the locations in a system where the Kernel will look for files. If a directory is not listed in your $PATH, the Kernel will not find it when you try to execute it.
5. Network Filesystem.
6. Journaled Filesystem.
7. The df command displays information about mounted filesystems.
8. An inode holds information about files like the size of a file; the UID of the file's owner; the GID of the file's owner; a unique identification number, called an inode number; the file's permission mode; some timestamps indicating when the inode was changed last, known as the (ctime); when the content of the file was last modified, known as the (mtime); and when the file was last accessed, known as the (atime); and a counter that keeps track of how many links are pointing to the inode.
9. echo $HOME or env | grep HOME or set | grep HOME or cd then pwd.
10. df –i for all mounted filesystems or df –i filesystem name for a specific filesystem.

5 – Solutions for Users, Groups, and Permissions Exercises

1. more /etc/passwd
2. du –hs /home/username
3. passwd
4. groups or more /etc/group or Do a long listing of a file you have made.
5. more /etc/group
6. touch gfile or chmod 774 gfile
7. chgrp staff oldgroup
8. touch .profile
9. MYNAME to your first name in your .profile or MYNAME=Joe (Your First Name) or export MYNAME or echo $MYNAME
10. PS1="$MYNAME@`uname -n`:\${PWD}> " export PS1

6 – Solutions for bash - The Bourne-Again Shell Exercises

1. echo $SHELL or env | grep SHELL or set | grep SHELL
2. /etc/shells
3. /etc/passwd or .profile
4. There is no limit
5. exit or Ctrl c key sequence.
6. &&
7. echo {p,h,t}en
8. LSCOLORS
9. Job Control
10. Bash

7 – Solutions for Managing Processes Exercises

1. ps
2. ps –f
3. ps –e or ps –A (Depending on your version of UNIX or Linux.)
4. PPID stands for Parent Process Identifier.
5. You can end a process that you own with the kill or pkill commands.
6. The -9 option when used with the kill command will force it to end even if it has child processes that are still running. Doing this will orphan the child processes and may create zombie processes. However, there are occasions when it is necessary to force a process to end.
7. A process that will not die is referred to as a *zombie process*. Technically when a process is in the zombie state, it isn't really a process anymore; rather, it is just an entry in the process table. It takes almost no system resources. The only real effect it has is that it clutters up the ps output, which is a pain for people trying to look at process information.
8. The best way to get rid of processes that will not die or zombie processes is to reboot the server.
9. Root
10. Your terminal session will close and you will be disconnected from the server.

8 – Solutions for Miscellaneous UNIX Utilities Exercises

1. bc, then scale=2, then 100/3
2. Ctrl d
3. cal 7 1776
4. date
5. date 011503452025
6. sar -r
7. uptime
8. Number of system CPUs
9. wc -l
10. r

9 - Solutions for Comparing, Sorting, and Compressing Exercises

1. diff file1 file2 or comm File1 file2 or cmp file1 file2
2. cmp file1 file2
3. sort –M months
4. sort –k 5 file1
5. sort –r file1
6. gzip filename original_file
7. gunzip file1.gz
8. tar cvf dir1.tar /dir1
9. tar tvf dir1.tar
10. tar xvf dir1.tar

10 – Solutions for Backup Exercises

1. Tape archive
2. It displays the tape of contents for the archive file.
3. It displays a dot for each file that can be used as a progress indicator.
4. It creates a list or table of contents.
5. dd
6. mt
7. Rewind and then take the tape device offline.
8. 2
9. Day of the Week
10. crontab –l (The "l" means list or look).

ABOUT THE AUTHOR

Robert Fay has worked in the IT industry for 20 years as a programmer analyst, systems administrator, storage area network (SAN) administrator, and client server network architect. During that time, he has had the opportunity to work with many different operating systems, including UNIX and Linux. The scope of UNIX and Linux flavors include AIX, CentOS, Fedora, HPUX, Knoppix, RHEL, SCO, Solaris, SuSE, and Ubuntu. He has supported UNIX and Linux on AMD, Compaq, HP, Intel, RISC, and SPARC architecture hardware. Over the years, he has had the opportunity to teach UNIX and networking classes to fellow employees as well as college students as a trainer and adjunct instructor. When he is not working with UNIX and Linux, he likes to work on home electronics and robotics projects.

www.ingramcontent.com/pod-product-compliance
Lightning Source LLC
Chambersburg PA
CBHW071153050326
40689CB00011B/2098